THE AMAZING
OVERSIGHT

For Linda

Best of luck

Ben

THE AMAZING OVERSIGHT

Total Participation for Productivity

EDITED BY

Ben S. Graham, Jr.
Parvin S. Titus

amacom

A Division of American Management Associations

This book was set in Souvenir Light by Vail-Ballou Press
It was designed by Dick Granald, LMD
Printer and binder were Vail-Ballou Press

Library of Congress Cataloging in Publication Data

Main entry under title:
The amazing oversight.

Includes bibliographies and index.
1. Employees' representation in management—
Addresses, essays, lectures. 2. Industrial productivity
—Addresses, essays, lectures. I. Graham, Ben S.
II. Titus, Parvin S.
HD5650.A475   658.31'52   79-10070
ISBN 0-8144-5510-7

© 1979 AMACOM
A division of American Management Associations, New York.
All rights reserved. Printed in the United States of America.

First Printing

The demand of management in a future filled with an increasing quantity and complexity of change will be for adequate measures designed to manage improvement more effectively. Improvement management as a prime concern of managers on every level will rest on a deeper understanding of people. This understanding will be expressed in a managerial attitude that supports and sustains the improvement process.

Through improvement management, executives may find a new future, a new look, and a new approach to their future responsibilities. They may find the way to live successfully with uncertainty.

Leo B. Moore
"How to Manage Improvement"
Harvard Business Review
July—August 1958

Preface

The Amazing Oversight is a reader dealing with the subject of job improvement through worker participation, a concept essential to the application of Work Simplification. This volume is made up of writings by the founders and pioneers of participative improvement and members of the International Advisory Board of the Improvement Institute, an organization established in 1967 as the International Work Simplification Institute. The book is essentially a statement of where this profession came from and what it is all about.

The practice of Work Simplification involves the organized application of common sense to find better, easier, and more effective ways of doing work. Essentially it is working smarter—not harder—by using the good sense of people who have first-hand experience aided by various charting and diagramming techniques to organize the facts. The beliefs underlying this practice are set forth in the official Creed of the Improvement Institute.

> We, the Improvement Institute, believe:
>
> *Quality of Work*—unconditionally in the ability of people to bring experience, judgment, and creativity to their work; and that people with first-hand experience must be involved in establishing and maintaining their methods of work if we are to have organizations and a society which are in touch with reality.
>
> *Education*—in the importance of life-long education to help people to live as closely as possible to their full potentials; and that it is important that education include a working knowledge of participation, involvement, and creativity.

Unions—in working harmoniously with the organizations chosen by the people.

Management—that every person is a manager; and that interpersonal confidence and trust are the keys to effective management.

Inflation—that prices and wages should not rise unless commensurate value is increased as well.

Consumers—that consumers should continuously receive better products and services at lower costs.

Resources—that we should support constructive efforts to conserve and efficiently recycle resources.

Community—that organizations should strive to become an acceptable and beneficial part of the communities where they are located.

Government—that organizations should work harmoniously with their government while supporting constructive efforts to improve its responsiveness and effectiveness.

The book is arranged in two parts, with the work of the pioneers describing the roots of the profession in the first part. The second part contains contributions of some of the newer leaders in the field.

The editors wish to express their appreciation for the contributions of all those whose work appears herein. Also to the other members of the International Advisory Board and Trustees of the Improvement Institute for their encouragement. Particular thanks are due to Ann Counts for her many hours of typing the manuscript, to R. W. Ford for its reproduction, and to Morley G. Melden for special assistance.

Ben S. Graham, Jr.
Parvin S. Titus

Contents

PART TWO
Current Trends
and Directions

Introduction

One of the most important issues of today involves the productivity—or rather the lack of it—in our organizations. At the same time the most highly educated workforce the world has ever known brings to the workplace an enormous reserve of talent which is largely going untapped.

Many individuals and groups have agonized over this situation and, with the best intentions, have undertaken programs to correct it. Unfortunately their well-intended efforts have often failed to produce any improvement. Some have even aggravated the situation.

It seems to be generally agreed that the quality of working life and the degree of involvement which people bring to their work are critical concepts. From there the approaches to achieving progress in these areas vary greatly, depending on the theories and biases of the proponents.

Meanwhile there is a tested body of knowledge in this field. Spawned in the fertile minds of outstanding pioneers and steadily tested and sharpened through decades of experience, this body of knowledge has become a primary factor accounting for massive productive accomplishments.

However, despite the magnitude of the results produced by this body of knowledge, it remains rather obscure, known well by only a relatively small number of practitioners.

The little that has been written by these people has had relatively little exposure, often faring badly in competition with more glamorous approaches to productivity improvement. Exotic new concepts, though untested, have become extremely popular.

Meanwhile, behind the scenes, people who share this body of knowledge continue to produce results day after day, year in, year out.

This book represents a careful attempt to assemble the best of the writings of those who planted the seeds and cultivated this field.

PART ONE
Pioneers

Challenge
of Viewpoint

Erwin H. Schell *Erwin H. Schell (1889–1965), a 1912 graduate of MIT, returned there after World War I for a teaching career that spanned over 40 years. He also served as a consultant and contributed many new management concepts and techniques. His belief in the worker's ability to help solve the problems of management led logically to many modern participative management practices.*

No one is at fault. No one is to blame. Indeed, if anyone should have seen it, we educators were the ones. We have not been so enmeshed in the urgent details of industry as have the industrialists. Our noses were farther from the grindstone. But we did not see it.

When we left our trains at their stations and passed down the platforms alongside the moguls or the great diesels with the men in blue denim caps up in the cabs, we should have seen it. But we did not.

When we stood on the bridge of the transatlantic liner, watching the man in the wheelhouse, we should have seen it. But we did not.

When we climbed into the air cruiser and saw the glint of the sun on the buttons and braid of the pilots as they went forward

Reprinted by permission of the publisher from *Motivating the Employee on Today's Production Front* (#203 in the AMA Manufacturing Series).©1952 by AMACOM, a division of American Management Associations. This article was originally published as "Industry's Amazing Oversight."

to the maze of dials around their perches in the forward quarters, we certainly should have had an inkling of the truth. But it never seemed to enter our minds.

Certainly, when we looked at the lines of cars speeding daily along the highways; when we watched the neighborhood handy man behind the power lawn mower; when we followed in the mirror the peregrinations of our barber's electric clippers; I really don't see how we could have missed it. But we did.

AN IMPERCEPTIBLE TREND?

Perhaps it was because the change had taken place gradually. Sometimes trends are so deliberate that we do not recognize small changes until something focuses our attention upon their accumulation.

I think of a New England factory that had expanded from a peacetime enrollment of 400 to 12,000 hands during World War I. As I was standing in the president's office, an elderly attendant who drove him back and forth between his home and his office entered.

"What can I do for you, Henry?" asked the president.

"Got to have some help, Mr. Butler. Ain't as strong as I used to be."

"What do you need help with, Henry?"

"It's the big satchel with the silver in it, Mr. Butler. I can't lift it up into the buggy any longer. Been lifting it for the last forty years, Mr. Butler, getting the payroll from downtown and bringing it out to the plant. But the nickels and the dimes and the quarters have been getting awful heavy lately."

The mathematics was simple. Here were 12,000 employees, averaging better than $1.00 an hour for, say, a 50-hour week. Here was the $600,000 payroll, coming down the mile-long street in an open buggy. The situation had just crept up unawares. And only by the grace of Providence had no one crept up on Henry!

6

A FAULTY PRECONCEPTION?

Perhaps we started off on the wrong foot in our thinking. As Elihu Thompson used to say, the greatest enemy of thought is the preconception, for when this preliminary assumption is in error, it curses our entire thinking forever after, no matter how high the quality of that thinking. For example, back in the old days, when bosses cracked bullwhips in the fields, and even earlier, when slaves bent to the oars of triremes, human relations were governed by the preconception of a basic difference in people—a difference that really was not there.

EARLY INKLINGS

I gained my first hint of this amazing oversight when comparing the content of two conferences that were held in a prosperous metal-working plant. Top management was planning meetings for foremen on the one hand, and for skilled machine operators on the other. At the first meeting we discussed the range of the foreman's responsibilities. Among other requirements, we specified that we must be production-conscious, cost-conscious, and quality-conscious. Then, within the hour, came the second conference, where the content of a booklet suitable for new trainees was being discussed. And included in this was the statement: These men, in addition to training in the mechanical process, should be taught the importance of being production-conscious, cost-conscious, and quality-conscious.

The identical note of these responsibilities was so striking that anyone would have recognized it. Yet still another experience was necessary before the idea began to form in my mind that here was a fundamental principle, which we had, in some unbelievable fashion, overlooked.

I was at the home of the superintendent of a large New Hampshire textile mill late one evening after a dinner and an address to his overseers. While we were discussing the sometimes curious behavior of workmen, the superintendent told this story.

In one department of the mill, a group of 40 employees operated somewhat complex machinery. Each man was permanently assigned to a single piece of equipment. None of the operators spoke English except the overseer, who on this particular afternoon was absent. Suddenly, when everything seemed to be going well, the workmen shut off their machines, left the plant, and made across the field to the town—all with much conversation. No one could make out the trouble, and the superintendent telephoned the village priest, asking his aid.

Shortly the priest reported: "These men all say you have taken their machines away from them. They say they have run these machines for many years, that they are *their* machines, and that now they have been taken away by the engineer."

Upon inquiry, the industrial engineer reported that, during the installation of a new work-assignment system, employees were being shifted about, depending upon machine-load factors, and were no longer assigned to a single facility. When word was sent to the operators that their machines would be returned to them until the situation could be restudied, they promptly returned to their work.

IS THE MACHINE OPERATOR MORE THAN A WORKER?

Slowly the question took form. Could it be that machine operators perform a kind of management? True, they do not manage people; but do they not, in reality, manage machines?

Of course there is a difference. In machine management, the incentive for increased tempo may come out of an oil can rather than a payment plan; whereas in managing people, a knowledge of human motives and "drives" is essential.

I remembered how the country schoolteacher scolded her class of young farm boys for hesitating as she asked them, "If a dog can run four miles an hour, how far would he run in two hours?" and how at last one little fellow exclaimed, "But, teacher, you haven't told us yet what that dog is chasing!"

Looking further, I consulted various lists of foremen's attributes and responsibilities and found them to include such major divisions as employee relations, quality, costs and budgets, meeting production schedules, equipment maintenance, working conditions, accident prevention, leadership, knowledge and skill, dependability and judgment, initiative and creativeness, and good health.

As I scanned this sequence of requirements, I thought to myself:

Should machine operators, as well as foremen, be skilled in *employee relations?* I recalled the statement of an older counselor who said: "When you go to work for any company, you must fit the job and, more important, fit the organization." Yes, employees have important employee relations.

Should machine operators be concerned with *quality?* I thought of the great shops in Detroit, where the employees give as much attention to gauging the product in process as to maintaining output. Yes, employees, in the last analysis, are at the basis of quality output.

Should machine operators share the responsibility of meeting *cost standards and budgets?* I remembered the budget expert who remarked: "No budget is any better than the faith of the executives and employees in it." Yes, employees have a definite responsibility here.

Should machine operators characteristically be interested in *meeting production schedules?* I knew at once the answer to this question—"Just ask the employee who falls behind the schedule." Yes, employees are inevitably interested.

Should machine operators, no less than foremen, accept responsibility for *equipment maintenance?* Over and over, I had heard the principle that the basis of preventive maintenance is to be found in the presence of alert, responsible employees, who report incipient difficulties before machine breakdowns occur. Yes, employees are inseparably related to maintenance control.

Should machine operators be properly concerned with main-

9

taining suitable *working conditions?* I could think of no factor closer to the operator's personal interest, except possibly the quality of his supervision. Conditions at the workplace profoundly affect the kind of *living* an operator enjoys at his work.

Should machine operators be actively involved in *accident prevention?* Here again I found the success of safety programs largely pivoting upon the degree to which safeguards are accepted and used by the employees. Yes, employees should shoulder a large share of responsibility for accident prevention.

Should we expect machine operators to exercise any so-called *leadership functions?* There came to mind a talk I once had with a plant executive about the numerous recreational activities of his employees and how he told me: "The greatest value of these many organizations run by employees is that they provide the seedbeds from which our future executives sprout." And everyone knows how frequently machine operators are asked to train newcomers, particularly in times when production is expanding rapidly. Yes, machine operators may often assume leadership.

Does the work of the machine operator normally involve *knowledge and skill?* I remembered the first time I worked on a high-speed grinder and how little help I felt my college diploma to be at the moment. I remembered an industrialist who said: "Watch out when the work looks easy. The chances are that you are observing a highly skilled operator who makes hard tasks look simple."

Should the virtues of *dependability and judgment* be looked for especially in the machine operator? I thought of the older workers, with many years of service, whom I had known. Every one of them had demonstrated these qualities in large measure.

Is there a need for the machine operator with *initiative and creativeness?* I turned back in my mind to the many company suggestion plans I had known; to the extraordinary stress given creative talents in employee-training programs with particular reference to methods; to the important place initiative and ingenuity hold in any list of factors leading to promotion. Surely, employees are increasingly expected to show initiative and creativeness.

Does *good health* properly rank high among operators no less than among executives? I recalled the machine operators along the tautly operated production lines that I had seen in the Midwest. Certainly, physical reliability always has been of importance to the American worker.

As I reviewed my answers to these questions, the conviction increased that there is far more similarity than difference between the so-called managerial requirements of the modern machine operator and those of the supervisor.

IS MACHINE MANAGEMENT TO BE FOUND ONLY IN THE FACTORY?

But what about those employees—men and women—whose work does not involve machine operation? Are they without managerial fitness? Or may they, in spite of the absence of factory production equipment, qualify in some measure as managers? With these immediate questions in mind, I became aware of a trend that is perhaps the most extraordinary of our time— the growth of machine management outside the factory walls.

Today there is scarcely a household in this country in which machine management is not practiced in one form or another. The automobile, the refrigerator, the washing machine, and the vacuum cleaner are only a few examples of the vast congeries of home equipment, the competent operation of which has called heavily upon the bedrock principles of good management.

It should be relatively easy to prove that there is as much if not more opportunity for the display of managerial skills in consumer, as opposed to production, activities. And it should not be difficult to find numerous companies in which the total company capital invested in machinery is actually less than the total employee capital invested in the automobiles found daily in their parking lots. In fact, someone has recently quipped that the American industry with the deepest potential reservoir of skilled labor is that in which the operators' duties most closely approximate the operation and maintenance of a fifth-hand motor car!

How profoundly Karl Marx erred in picturing man as the slave of the machine! Today man as never before—in his work, his home, his play—is the acknowledged master of the mechanisms he employs. Machines have made men free.

ARE MANAGERIAL SKILLS SOLELY THE PRODUCT OF THE FACTORY?

Looking closer, I found an even broader area for the application of managerial skills. People in private life are also managers. The planning and maintenance of gardens, of hobbies, and of neighborhood committees all call for management on the part of the householder.

Nor can we overlook the special province of the housewife. The home has long since emerged from the master-and-servant status and has assumed its place as an environment suitable for the highest development of human cooperation and personality. The term "home manager" has for many years received wide acceptance. . . .

As the picture came more sharply into focus, I realized that management is not, at base, a matter of occupation—of machines, of jobs, of work. I realized that it marks a stage of life; that there comes a time in every human being's existence—frequently upon leaving the parental home—when he or she is no longer managed. That is when self-management begins. Moreover, management is an attitude of mind that has vigorously rebelled against enclosure in any given social or industrial stratum.

Suddenly it has become evident that management is a widely pervasive form of social activity—a kind of doing that is in no way the perquisite of any single class—and that management is an inherent ingredient in the lives of every one of us.

WHAT HAS BEEN HAPPENING TO OUR INDUSTRIAL WORKERS?

What has been happening in and out of our factories and mills? Unnoticed, a great body of equipment managers has been accumulating throughout our industries and our communities.

12

Without herald or fanfare, the increasing transfer of skill and effort to the machine—whether in the workplace, in the home, or on the highway—has in turn developed new qualities of managerial proficiency in those who put these engineries through their daily paces.

We can now understand why, in the past, plant policies that have stifled or obstructed managerial activities normally open to the operator have been the basis of frustrations, maladjustments, and tensions in the working group. For example, paternalists who insisted on managing personal affairs for their workers promptly encountered resentment. We all must manage something, if it is only our own lives.

Most important, we now can see no further reason for giving obeisance to that imaginary and ever-troublesome line that, since the days of the medieval master and servant, has been drawn between manager and worker. At last we see that the responsibilities of people employed in industry differ in degree but not in kind. Basically we are all alike. Management is not confined to any sector of industry. It is a pervasive, all-embracing responsibility.

We need not wait for slow evolution to bring an end to industrial discord and class enmity. Before our very eyes are legions of experienced *work managers* who, if given proper recognition as authentic parts of the management team, will profit greatly from increased self-respect and contribute immensely to the welfare and progress of their industry.

Here we have both an amazing oversight and a stupendous opportunity, pointing the way to the direct application of that principle of human equality and interdependence on which security for the free world rests.

WHAT HAS BEEN HAPPENING TO OUR EXECUTIVES AND SUPERVISORS?

I looked at what is happening on the executive and administrative levels above the operator or worker to verify the soundness of my line of reasoning. I found that:

13

1. We are seeing the steady and purposeful delegation of authority and responsibility downward.
2. We are seeing the decentralization of effort to afford responsibility within the span of control of the supervisor.
3. We are seeing the arousing of *esprit* and morale by a clearer understanding of the basis upon which American industry has been built and the climate in which it best operates.
4. We are seeing the growing importance of clearly drawn avenues of communication up and down the executive structure—of well-established organizational relationships.
5. Finally, we are seeing the widespread acceptance of the principle that cooperation in the doing springs best from participation in the planning.

May these activities not be extended with equal benefit to employees who are at close grips with the basic operative tasks, which are the primary justification for the enterprise?

Is there not great advantage in awakening a keen sense of company responsibility among our worker group, no less than among our supervisors?

Is there not value for the employee in a program that, through decentralization, permits a clearer understanding of the whole job?

Is not a deeper and more widespread appreciation of the American way of industrial life as essential to the worker as to the executive?

Does not good communication continue to multiply benefits as it is extended to the productive employee?

Is there not growing proof that employee participation in planning can and will bring far-reaching benefits in cooperation?

WHAT HAS BEEN HAPPENING TO INDUSTRY?

We may again judge the soundness of our thesis by examining its pertinence in relation to current industrial trends. For example, we know that in the future the actual toil of industry—the expenditure of brawn—will increasingly be transferred to the machine. When we ask, "What shall we pay employees to do 50 years from now?" we are certain that we shall not be paying them for hard physical labor. We shall be paying them for equipment and process management.

Again, we know that rates of technological advance and improvement will be further accelerated as we learn to avoid unemployment or inflation. Clearly, we shall not be able to accomplish these desired ends without capitalizing creatively upon that experience in operating details that only a complete camaraderie can release.

We know that industry as a social institution will focus attention sharply upon the task of improving the self-reliance, self-confidence, and self-initiative of its worker personnel, in order to bring these abilities to a point at least equal to that now provided by other major vocations—for example, agriculture. This can result only when employees are given wider opportunity for self-development in the business of machine management, job management, and self-management.

We anticipate that the power of financial incentives will steadily wane. Obviously, new forms of human satisfaction must be provided if we are to maintain the advantages of private enterprise. Foremost among these is the satisfaction that comes with truly belonging to the group, with becoming dedicated to a common cause. . . .

WHAT ACTION SHOULD FOLLOW?

The wish to participate in the direction, guidance, and control—in short, in the management—of affairs is one of the deepest desires of man. The machine and the technical process in factory and home have provided effective vehicles for the satisfaction of this basic urge and for the development of skills in managerial techniques.

May industry set about building a new and mighty unity on the basic principle that all men of industry, whether officials or operators, from president to lowliest employee, are in varying degree executives in their own right.

May industry recognize and act upon the opportunity to close its ranks over and across that obsolete remnant of earlier days and earlier ways—that artificial abyss of class distinction which has heretofore separated management and labor.

Why should it have taken us so long to see these changes developing over the years before our very eyes? How can we explain our amazing oversight? I think of the old saying of the Pennsylvania Dutch: "Ve grow so soon old, und so late schmardt!"

How
It All Started

Allan H. Mogensen

Allan H. Mogensen, sometimes called the "Father of Work Simplification," developed that philosophy as a result of his experiences as a teacher at the University of Rochester and as a working engineer at Eastman Kodak. As a consultant to the Secretary of War during World War II, he applied Work Simplification techniques in defense industries and in several combat theaters. His Leadership Conferences, which began in 1937, continue today.

What has come to be known as Work Simplification started when I was teaching industrial engineering at the University of Rochester in the late 1920s. During the summer months I worked in various Rochester industries, making time studies and setting rates. However, it was not until I worked in the industrial engineering department at Eastman Kodak and discovered the new 16mm camera and film just being introduced, that I felt certain that we industrial engineers were on the wrong trail.

THE IMPORTANCE OF METHOD

This came about in two ways. First, we were then arguing about the validity of Taylor's insistence that we study only the "first class man" as against the new concept promoted by Lowry, Maynard, and Stegemerten—that we separate skill and effort in

17

evaluating performance. Their principle of leveling no doubt had a great deal to do with taking time study out of disrepute, as it was usually regarded. No doubt it also had a lot to do with the development of predetermined time standards (which are so prevalent today).

However, the job of training time-study men to rate skill and effort was just in its infancy. In "Common Sense Applied to Motion and Time Study," published in 1932, I said: "We may in the future see films developed for just this purpose. Thus a new observer can be shown a film illustrating fair skill and excellent effort as contrasted with another operator who is superskilled but may be exerting only average effort." At that time I had built a 16mm projector with a speed counter attached, and was engaged in doing just this with my industrial engineering students.

I soon ran across a situation that threw me. We were rating the overall performance of an operator. I realized that if we were going to rate properly, we would have to break the operation down into variables and constants before we could evaluate performance.

Let me illustrate: Suppose we have an operator who picks up a part, raises it in the air—say on the right side of the workplace—then moves it over to the left side, and drops it. Now, we film that job. After processing, let's say that we run the projector first very slowly. We see the operator having great difficulty in grasping the part, slowly raising it in the air, slowly moving it over to the left, and then releasing it. On being released, the part slowly falls to the bench. Now let us speed up the projector to simulate the performance of a highly skilled worker, demonstrating maximum effort. We see the part picked up quickly, raised and carried over to the left rapidly, but then again the fallacy is evident: The part seems to fall in half the time we all know it will take, following the law of gravity. In other words, in one instance it takes twice as long as normal to fall, in the other it falls in half the time. Of course, we know that regardless of the skill or effort on the part of the operator, the time required for the part to fall is a constant.

18

The Man on the Job

It became evident to me that if we were to rate performance, we would have to separate the operations into variables and constants in order to set a proper standard. Then, as I took films of various operations in industry and offices, I realized that in the above example the really outstanding operator might snap the part quickly across the workbench, getting it there in a fraction of the time. Either through his analysis of the operation, or just through his natural desire to do it in the easiest way, he discovered that it was unnecessary to take the time to grasp the part, raise it in the air, and wait for it to drop. The movement from right to left was all that was required.

Now, if the first method is set up by the industrial engineer (I.E.) as the one to be followed, and a standard is set on the job, we are in real trouble. If the operator is on incentive, he has to figure out just how far he dare go in increasing output and how much money he dare make before the I.E. comes back and cuts the rate. So for all these years we have been trying to outsmart the workers under various incentive pay plans, and the result has been featherbedding, restriction of output, and limitation of production, for which we are paying dearly in poor productivity. I am certain, after half a century of industrial experience, the operator can always outsmart any I.E.

This led me to the conclusion that time study and rate-setting without a thorough study of the methods involved could lead only to disaster. This also led me to Dr. Lillian Gilbreth, and with her generous help I discovered all the work that she and Frank Gilbreth had done, not only in motion study, but in the human side of work and workers.

The second discovery I made about the "wrong trail" came about while we were making motion picture films of various operators in the camera works of Eastman Kodak one summer. Time and time again, we would shoot a job scene and the foreman would assure us that it was being performed according to proper practice. Later when he and the operator reviewed it on the screen, we received loud protestations. "Oh my gosh, we

19

can't let that film be seen. The method is terrible! Let us improve it, and please take the pictures over."

It was then doubly reinforced to me: first, that in the motion picture we had a new and powerful tool for improving methods, but far more important—that the operators often had many priceless ideas for improvement but very seldom were they ever consulted. At this turning point in my life, I came to the conclusion that *"the person doing the job knows far more than anyone else about the best way of doing that job, and therefore is the one person best fitted to improve it."*

All the rest is history. When I started the Work Simplification Conferences at Lake Placid in 1937, Dave Porter and I stressed the importance of the motion picture camera as an aid to improvement. Through the years, until 1966, training in the taking of excellent motion pictures was an important part of the experience of over 1,000 delegates.

In 1966, we pioneered in the use of videotape, which I regard today as the best training tool available in business and industry. At both our Sea Island Executive and Lake Placid Leadership Conferences, it has played an increasing part in our success.

Finally, I wish to pay tribute to Professor Erwin H. Schell, who asked me to lecture in his classes at MIT in 1931. In 1932, he suggested the name, "Work Simplification," which has described our philosophy so well for over 40 years.

Erwin Schell was on our staff at Lake Placid, Sea Island, and other conferences from the first one until his retirement. He had the unbelievable vision to see well down the road. In 1952 he presented his now famous paper, "Industry's Amazing Oversight." This lecture was one of his outstanding contributions to our conferences, but I am ashamed to say that, although we thought we realized its import, few of us really did. Dr. M. Scott Myers, in "Every Employee a Manager," published in 1970, substantiated through meaningful research everything that Erwin Schell had foreseen. As Schell said in his paper, "Ve grow so soon old, und so late schmardt!"

Management's Place in the World Today

Lillian M. Gilbreth

Lillian M. Gilbreth (1878–1972), working with her husband, Frank (1868–1924), and on her own, contributed much to the development of motion economy and its application to increasing productivity in industry and in the home.

In addressing "Management's Place in the World Today," I want to stress especially the word "world," because I think now is the time we have to expand our thinking to include the whole world. In some ways it may seem like a smaller world to us because we can get around so rapidly. But in many ways it is a wider world because our interests stretch as far as there are people facing problems. If in the management world we can make a world movement, have emphasis upon the things we believe in— freedom of choice, the right serviceable values—then management has done a good job. But if we preempt those values in this country, in any other country, in any group of countries, then of course we are not living up to the responsibilities given to us.

The management movement in this country was started by a group of men who were all engineers, and therefore one might think that the emphasis would be put primarily upon technical values, but that wasn't the case. What was the goal of this

Feature address before the 25th Progress Review, Work Simplification Conference, Lake Placid Club, July 7, 1961. Published by the *Journal of Industrial Engineering,* Special Report, pp. SR 40–43, May 1962.

group? What is the goal, not only of engineers, but of all people who are trying to work for world betterment? They said very simply that they thought it was their goal, their job, to utilize the resources of nature and human nature for the benefit of mankind. Now that final clause "for the benefit of mankind" is the difficult one because who is to decide what is for the benefit of mankind? All we can do is to try to think carefully as to what that might be and do our best to further things in that direction. It is quite obvious that we have succeeded very well in utilizing the resources of nature. As one goes over the field of the natural sciences; as one sees the older men, but especially the young men and women coming into the field; as we hear about those in the colleges and universities and what they are electing to do, and the young people preparing for college and what they wish to do—we can see that the development of the resources of nature is very well in hand.

When it comes to the development of human nature, I think there too our record is fairly good, but we have to keep our eyes constantly on the picture to make sure that those resources are utilized. It is encouraging that this emphasis on the resources of nature and using them for the betterment of mankind has been a stimulus to what we feel has been one of the great growths in the field of management—that is, inviting people of all backgrounds, not only of all countries, races, and religions, but people of all disciplines (the exact sciences, the social sciences, and the arts)—to come into the picture, to advise together just how this development can be done so that we shall truly make, not only in quantity but in quality, all the contribution we can. When you realize that in the early days we did have engineers and people in the natural sciences but really very few in the social and human sciences, you see how necessary it was that the latter group and all its representatives be asked to take part. Now that wasn't because the pioneers or the people in the field of natural sciences were not kindly, were not humanitarian, but that there was not available at that time the fine development that came later in the field of the human sciences.

I have always been so happy over the name "Work Simplification" because it seems to me that besides all of the other tangible things it has done, it has given a more positive, creative value to the word "work." Work, which used to be thought a curse by some people, necessarily involved drudgery, something which you did very quickly in order to go to something else. It took perhaps that awful time of unemployment, when people did not have work to do, to make us realize that work was a blessing, that work was something for which we should be thankful, to which we should look forward, prepare for with joy, do with joy. (I think perhaps along with unemployment in general, we have to say a word about the kind of unemployment that has come to many people who have been retired from opportunities and jobs before they wanted to be and—unless they had the enrichment of experience, or society had the forethought to get ready to make them feel that they were wanted and needed—might very well feel that they were denied work and that a blessing had fallen out of their lives.)

I liked, too, the word "Simplification," because I think after years of debate, we have decided that almost anybody can make things complex, but to take something which is complex and to make it simple—that is a great achievement. I think of the various groups who have joined us in this field—the physiologists, the psychologists, and now the sociologists and psychiatrists. They came to work with us, who by and large had a very simple vocabulary and were very pleased about that. This has led many of them to simplify their own vocabulary so that in these days when you hear a speaker or read the things being written in that field, unless they are writing for each other (when any group has a right to use jargon), try to use the common simple tongue which we intend to hold on to in our Work Simplification area. We feel it is an asset, not a liability.

Some of these sciences, and psychiatry in particular, have been able to help us in seeing fundamental reasons and depths to problems that perhaps we would not have otherwise seen. So we feel great gratitude as we plan for the world-wide expansion of our concepts. It is a wonderful thing to find that we may have a considerable amount to give but we have a very great deal to gain and I think it is a joy as you look over the past and around at the present and toward the future to know that in all of these groups we have so much to offer other countries. Once we learn easy, free communications back and forth, we shall have a group that can work easily and happily together.

Now, as you all know, the method we use is the questioning method and of all the questions, *why* stands out as the most important. That should be a great asset to us as we go out to the other groups who are now working in the industrial field, and say, "See, it is your help that gives us this emphasis on the *why,* and we hope you will continue to remind us constantly that *why* is the eternal question; so that as we continue it today, but tomorrow we pick it up again, and we say it may have been so yesterday, but *why* is it so today and so on indefinitely into the future."

I think it is just as well we started in industry and business (especially in these days when we know that industry and business mean so much to the entire world). It is important to us that our own industry and business should flourish, not only because of what they give us all, but because of what we can give because of them. Business and industry do so much for the welfare of the people of all countries be they developed or so-called underdeveloped (which I like to call "young-in-development") countries. . . . We know that only as they can take over their own responsibilities and solve their own problems are they going to have freedom and feel that they are in the position to handle their own affairs; and it is more than that, it is the great desire that they all have, not only to get but to give. . . .

From business and industry, of course, we went to the office, we went to the farm, and gradually branched out until now there is a tremendous amount of interest in hospitals, libraries, work with the physically disabled—every area where work is going on, there management can go. There we can find how we can use what we know or could know about the what, and the who, and the where, the when and how and the why. For a long time, I think, Europe and the other countries of the world thought the important thing was the *how*. The Americans knew how, and of course, the know-how is important. . . . So many of our men who were engineers or had other training have had that first-hand participation out on a job.

I never will forget going into the Orient many years ago and visiting a beautiful factory. Everything had been swept up to the point that even the coal, which they were burning in those days, had been removed while the visitors were there. It wasn't a natural environment; it was just like a house all scrubbed up to the point that the family comes in and says, "Well, I see we have the best china today." Something happened to the machine we were watching and the man who was there sent for somebody; he came and he sent for somebody else. He started to send for somebody else; and one of our young men took off his coat and simply went over to the machine and fussed with it a bit and the machine started. In an Oriental country at that time this situation could have caused a loss of status and embarrassment to the individuals involved. However, the way it was handled, the man who repaired the machine gained status for himself, his profession, his country, and his group, because he could actually do something about it. That feeling of carrying with you what can be done and demonstrating how it can be done has been a tremendous asset as we have gone into other countries. . . . Even in our own country, among our own people, where things are so highly developed, you really need somebody who knows how to do the job and does do the job with the learners. And it is even more true of these "young-in-development" countries. People whom we send out from the management and other fields, if they have that kind of know-how along with the training and technical background, it means something very different. That, too, I like to think, is a world aspect of management.

Now, how about the applications in a human being's life— your life or mine? We are all management people whether we know it or not, because every one of us has four or five areas where we more or less have to manage and where we might just as well recognize it and see what is available to help us. Area number one, I think, is managing ourselves. Now that is the least considered area; it is often the forgotten area. Many people are ready and glad to undertake managing anybody, any group, any project, but they never think that perhaps they need some management, some self-management. And really, until they come to the point where they can manage themselves, they are not going to be permanently an asset in the management field. . . . I am sorry to tell you that some of the most brilliant people in the management field, and some of them very successful top management, really never learn to manage themselves. . . .

The second one, of course, is the home and the family. I think business and industry, management in particular, is learning more and more how important the home is. We have known for a long time it's the big market. Most of the buying is done for the home or by the home manager, but it is more than that. It is the center of education, the center of serenity. In business or industry you know perfectly well that no matter how well you try to have good working conditions, if people come from homes where the housekeeping is poor and the family relations are unhappy, there is nothing you can do in the other fields. The teacher in the school, the superintendent in the shop, the manager all know that kind of thing. On the other hand, we know that if our people come from homes and families where the housekeeping is good, and the family relations are happy, we can weather a lot of difficult problems in the other fields. . . .

Our greatest contribution is the work that has been done with the physically disabled homemaker and especially the young one who has polio or some other disabling disease and perhaps is in a wheelchair for the rest of her life. She may have crutches or prosthetic devices of one kind or another, but she wants to go on keeping house, she wants to go on having a family and taking care of her family and being attractive and young. The University of Connecticut has for years been working with these young women. It is not only surprising what can be done from the management standpoint to make their lives easier, but it is astonishing to me that these young women are willing to be photographed and studied and the results shared with people everywhere, so that other young women who have calamities may see that things can be done.

The next group I think of is the citizen type of job. You all know the things that citizens do these days. Some of them are really touching and remarkable. I always think of President Hoover, a young boy who worked his way through college and married a fine girl, became a mining engineer, and went to China. They decided they didn't need a great deal. Just as soon as they had enough for a comfortable living and security, they wanted to use their lives for the benefit of mankind. He never took a nickel from the government for all the various jobs done. We don't all have the capacity, the devotion, but there are a number of citizen jobs being done all over this country—all over the world—where management can be of use and is being used.

I don't know whether the volunteer job is another division as you can be a volunteer on any job, but I do think it has been amazing to see the change in many volunteer jobs which has come about as management in general and perhaps Work Simplification in particular has come into the picture. . . . The improvement has been wonderful. You know now what is to be done, when, how, and why it is to be done, and the kind of person and traits that are needed. I like the kind of jobs an imaginative group can do for a community as a volunteer activity. One of our groups went to a city government and asked if they didn't want their jobs analyzed. The government didn't especially want these analyses done, although it thought it needed them. In any event, the job was done painlessly. . . .

I remember when some engineers came to our town, went to the library, looked at the books, and said that they thought many of the books were outmoded and that there were better books. Our clever librarian immediately said, "Gentlemen, this is just what I have been needing. Will your society please take over the job of reading our books and sorting them for us, and we will gladly dispose of any and will buy all our budget allows." She didn't say any more, but I am sure they realized that when the budget didn't quite meet the needs, perhaps volunteer contributions would help a little bit.

How about the international aspects? I think we get the feeling sometimes that we are more different from each other than we really are. Absolutely untrue: Human nature is human nature pretty much anywhere. We are much more alike everywhere than we were. We are getting organizations to help us, too. If you want to belong to a management group, there is one right in your own community where you are very welcome. If you belong to a local group then you belong to a state group and also to a national group. We have a good national group with headquarters in New York, and it is one of about thirty-odd groups all over the world who belong to the International Association. We have regular conferences, and had one in Mexico not long ago.

During the conference, I went to a supermarket. The man who ran the market came to the United States and studied everything our supermarkets had. He voided all the things we wished we didn't have and he carefully took down and evaluated all the things we thought were good and then he adapted them to the situations and the people of Mexico. I never saw better handling of food, from the time it came in one door, was processed and packaged, until it went out with the consumer. Again an indication that we have so much to learn as well as to give.

Then there is the European region, and we'd love to tell you about our Work Simplification people in Europe. One of the men who was here last year came from one of the companies that has sent us many men for these courses. He is now back in Europe and I saw him in Paris. He was starting his first course and he had 12 people in it from his company, each from a different country, and each primarily with the job of going through the Work Simplification course to see what changes needed to be made to make it adaptable to the country in which it is to be done, but being careful not to make changes of a sort which would mean that the groups from all over the world could not work comfortably together. . . .

"Life Long Learning," the motto of UCLA, it seems to me, is an appropriate motto for us. Every one of you is a manager, and now I tell you that you are a teacher, too. We have to learn all the time, we have to teach all the time, and there are so many things we have to teach. We have to teach that life is interesting,

28

we have to teach that life is worthwhile, and we have to teach that life ought to be beautiful. You remember it was a poet, not a prose writer, who wrote the loveliest things about teaching we know. It was Chaucer who said, "and first he wrought and afterwards he taught," as well as "and gladly would he learn and gladly teach." So what do we want? We want trained and educated people. We want educated heads in the very best way we know of educating. We want educated hands though I am not sure of their conserving and developing as they should; but if we say industry is not going to need so much of that sort of thing, how about the arts? Are we going to use the time we have to teach the arts and crafts and other things that not only produce beauty but provide an appreciation of beauty? Above all, of course, we need educated hearts. We need people who care. That provided, we shall have the emphasis on the human element we have been asking for, and I think that probably will give us peace so that we can as a world, using the tools that have been given us, go into our future unafraid.

Paperwork Simplification

Ben S. Graham, Sr.

Ben S. Graham, Sr. (1900–1960), one of the pioneers of the systems profession, adapted the work of Mogensen and the Gilbreths to the office environment by developing techniques for paperwork simplification. His innovations in clerical workplace design are widely used today.

FOUR BASIC PRINCIPLES

Paperwork has been in the spotlight since the early days of World War II. Following the war and a return to competitive markets, the emphasis on cost has led to many varied attempts to reduce paperwork and office non-productive costs. Too often the emphasis has been on the non-productive costs rather than on the elimination of waste. This misplaced emphasis can frequently lead to apparent cost reductions which result in expensive wastes in other areas.

Measurement of paperwork in terms of the objective—"does it help someone do his job better?"—can help in the elimination of much of the major "office" waste. It is also important to measure the values derived from the product of the paperwork, against the cost of that product. When this is done, systems important to the control of production, product quality, or cost will not be the unfortunate victims of an economy drive.

Ben S. Graham, *Work Simplification for Improved Business Controls and Operation of All Functions,* Chapter 1. Copyright © 1956 by the Standard Register Company. Reprinted by permission of The Standard Register Company and The Ben Graham Corporation.

Elimination of waste is our objective in Paperwork Simplification. This includes the waste due to entire procedures that do not measure up, the waste found in duplication of systems, poorly designed systems, inaccurate and low production in the various phases of a system. More important, it includes the waste which occurs in the productive functions of a business due to inaccurate or inadequate paperwork. Most important of all, Paperwork Simplification and Work Simplification take into account the waste of personal interest, initiative, and enthusiasm, and never overlook the importance of the acceptance of the improved method by the people who will use it.

WORK SIMPLIFICATION DEFINED

Paperwork Simplification is the adaptation of Work Simplification to the problems of paperwork. Work Simplification is defined in simple terms as, "The organized application of common sense to find better and easier ways of doing a job" or, as I prefer, "The organized application of common sense by everyone to eliminate waste of any kind—wasted time, energy, space, material, equipment, etc." *Eliminate waste* implies getting results, not just talking about it. Results come from better methods only when they are enthusiastically used by the people concerned. For years, the "enthusiastic use by the people concerned" was the reef on which many "better methods" foundered.

In the middle thirties several of the leaders in the field of scientific management—Allan Mogensen, Professor Erwin H. Schell of MIT, Dr. Lillian Gilbreth, and Professor David B. Porter of New York University—recognizing the importance of enthuasiastic cooperation, combined the simple fundamentals of the technique of motion study with a way of thinking or philosophy of management and called it Work Simplification. Having repeatedly developed and installed better methods only to return a few months later and find that people on the job had reverted to their old methods, these pioneers recognized the problem involved in developing *acceptance* of the better methods. The

31

problem involved the most difficult and highest types of selling, the selling of an idea or an intangible. People buy what they want rather than what is good for them or what they need.

The first and most important problem, then, is to convince the individual worker that he has a direct personal stake in eliminating every possible element of waste. Then get the individual "into the act" in the elimination of waste and he will "buy" his own ideas for improvement enthusiastically and make them work. Too often the expert mistakenly calls his activity "Work Simplification." In many cases anticipated results are not achieved because of the seeming lack of appreciation of the importance of enthusiastic cooperation on the part of every individual.

Today in Work Simplification and particularly Paperwork Simplification, it is extremely important that we integrate all the management and improvement techniques in their proper relationship for effective business operation. Techniques include scientific organization, delegation of responsibility, personnel selection, job evaluation, conference leadership, training, accounting, cost accounting, motion study, work measurement, mechanization, automation, integrated data processing, operations research, and the various psychological, sociological, and other techniques as they may apply in a given organization or situation. But they must be coordinated. Overemphasis on one destroys the balance and distorts results. Even more important, if they are to be accepted and used effectively by business, they must be reduced to simple terms understandable by management and by others not technically trained.

Productive Activity

The simple principles of Work Simplification provide a basic guide in the integration of these techniques, emphasize the importance of the individual, recognize the need for enthusiastic cooperation, and provide simple, usable measurement of the effectiveness of methods.

The first principle is: *Activities should be productive.* By "activ-

32

ity" we mean anything that goes on in business, including delays and storages, as well as the various operations and moves in a procedure. Since paperwork is entirely a nonproductive function of business, it is necessary to stretch the meaning of the word "productive" when we apply these principles to paperwork. However, many products of paperwork are essential to the best conduct of the business. If we define productivity as directly accomplishing the end results, we can apply the term to paperwork.

The typing of a three-part letter, an original and two copies, will illustrate the point. Assembling three sheets of paper and two sheets of carbon, jogging them into alignment, inserting them in the machine, positioning them in the machine, removing and separating them after the typing operation, are all nonproductive. The only productive part of the operation is the actual typing when the information is put on the paper. Long moves from desk to desk and delays on the desk are nonproductive elements in paperwork procedure. The first objective then is to reduce the nonproductive elements in our paperwork to an absolute minimum.

Smooth Flow

The second principle is: *Activity should be arranged to provide smooth flow from operation to operation in a process or a balanced motion pattern for an operator at a workplace.* Everybody knows how discouraging an unduly heavy workload can be to the average worker. Worrying about getting the work out distracts attention from the job at hand and slows up the actual production tremendously.

On the other hand, the average person is much happier when busy than when looking for work. This was illustrated very forcefully by an experience in the invoicing department in a large corporation. Application of Work Simplification, particularly the first principle, had cut the workload in half in the typing department. The typists who should have been released by this reduction in work were badly needed in another department. However, the supervisor, accustomed to being measured by an all-too-common standard of how many people he supervised, could only see his empire being cut in half. The typists, afraid that some of their group would be worked out of a job, stretched out the work to appear busy. Quality fell off, discord crept in, until the department was thoroughly disorganized. When half the women were finally transferred to other work, production more than doubled, quality rose to its highest level, and all the women, now honestly busy, were happier in their work. Smooth flow or balance is important especially in paperwork.

Simplicity

Our third principle is: *Activity should be as simple as possible.* In examining countless paperwork systems in business and industry, I have been reminded of Rube Goldberg's cartoons illustrating extremely complex and involved ways of accomplishing very simple results.

The study of a receiving system in an industrial plant illustrates how the simplifying of paperwork activity can also facilitate elimination of many elements of waste in productive functions. The objective of the system was to provide facts regarding thousands of items received, aid in control of the quantity and quality of materials received, facilitate the storage and prompt availability of the materials to the proper production department, relieve procurement of further responsibility, enable accounts receivable to pay for the materials, and help the cost and other departments carry out their functions. The old system, which had grown up over the years to meet varying requirements, included three separate forms which had to be written for each shipment (involving seven copies all together) and a ten-copy summary of all shipments received, which was used to advise the interested parties. Because the information had to be written four times, there were many errors in transcription and long delays before the summary could be completed. The laboratory, which was supposed to control the quality of many of the items received, frequently did

34

not receive its copy of the summary report until the items were already being used.

In many cases, department heads had to search through 30 or 40 items on the summary sheet to find whether or not the one item in which they were interested had been received. In the various accounting departments, the use of the summary report added substantially to their work and severely handicapped their functioning.

A simple eight-part form completed immediately after the receipt of the shipment eliminated rewriting the information three times, with the three opportunities for transcription errors; advised all interested parties promptly as to the receipt of each shipment; enabled the laboratory to test required items for quality before they had been used; and saved many hours of unnecessary work in the purchasing, production, and accounting departments.

As in this case, it is almost invariably true that simplification through elimination of waste improves not only production but quality as well.

These three principles covering the technique of Work Simplification are simple enough to be understood and used by the average person to measure the effectiveness of almost any work activity. These principles and the technique are, as can be seen, a simplified version of Motion Study. Contrary to many mistaken concepts, Motion Study as conceived by the Gilbreths is not limited to the activity of an individual at a workplace. One of the most important tools of Motion Study is the Flow-Process chart, a simple device for visualizing and measuring chronologically every detail in an overall process or procedure. It is, in reality, the "steam shovel" approach to the elimination of waste as compared with the "hand shovel" or "teaspoon" approach used in examining the individual operation. Each of the so-called laws, or methods, of making Motion Study effective, may be classified under one of the three principles.

As usual, we have three principles for the mechanics and only one left to cover the important part of Work Simplification—the human side. The emphasis must be in the opposite ratio. The human relation aspect is at least 75 percent of the job in Work Simplification.

Personal Interest

The fourth and, by far, most important principle is: *Participation with "know how," built on understanding, stimulates interest, initiative, and imagination, and results in enthusiastic cooperation.* The more the question is studied, the more apparent is the fact that the individual produces most effectively in terms of quantity, quality, and cost when personal satisfaction is derived from the job. Participation provides personal satisfaction when it is "built on understanding."

Understanding and confidence must permeate the organization from top to bottom. When this situation exists, participation in the elimination of waste will be carried on enthusiastically and will provide the opportunity for self-expression, accomplishment, and recognition; provide job interest; and develop enthusiastic cooperation. The individual, equipped with the technique and tools to eliminate waste and make improvements, has a tremendous satisfaction in initiating changes and developing better methods.

The change in attitude, the effective teamwork resulting from participation, is well expressed as, "the difference between enthusiastic cooperation and dignified acquiescence."

DEVELOPING PARTICIPATION IN PAPERWORK SIMPLIFICATION

One who is initiating Work Simplification—the leader himself and the coordinating committee which may have been appointed—will appreciate the primary importance of generating interest and enthusiasm from top to bottom. The value of "participation with know-how" in accomplishing the objectives cannot be emphasized too often.

Work Simplification—as the organized application of common sense by everyone to eliminate waste—is a continuing activity and should be part of everyone's job. It is a philosophy of cooperative activity to achieve a common objective in the most effective manner. Properly developed, it is an on-the-job climate or atmosphere of teamwork. If job evaluation or merit rating is used at any or all levels, effective participation in eliminating waste should be recognized as a factor in it.

Companywide participation should be the ultimate goal. But there are initially three approaches open to us. One is through top management on a companywide basis. The second is a departmental approach. And the third is through on-the-job training by the staff specialists. Let's review them.

Starting at the Top

A companywide approach must be predicated on a sound organizational setup—a proper delegation of responsibilities all the way down the line. It entails initial activity by top management to eliminate waste. Above all, it requires an appreciation by top management of the importance of people, the possibility for improvement through those people, and their need for the intangible satisfactions associated with their jobs.

What do we mean by top management waste elimination? Recently one company found that for requisitions of $100 or more, sixteen executive approvals were required on a five-part set. Since the set was not prefabricated with interleaved carbons, in many cases each executive signed five times, making a total of 80 signatures required. Obviously, this involved tremendous elements of waste and probably cost almost as much as the purchase of $100 worth of material. As long as such a situation existed at the top level, it would be extremely difficult to generate much interest at lower levels in eliminating relatively smaller elements of waste. It is important that top management people do more than give lip service to participation. They must act and let the results of their actions be known in order to arouse interest in the possibility of participation.

37

Spreading Interest

After top management has gotten into the act and produced results, the next step is to interest the next levels of management. An analysis of the problems facing the organization should provide the necessary material to arouse interest at each level. Problems such as increased competition, increased costs cutting into profit margins, and the need for continual improvement in product and cost to keep the company growing, all affect every member of an organization. However, these problems must be presented to the individuals in terms of their personal interests. Any one or all may be a threat to the job security of every individual in the company. This should not be used as a threat to generate participation but rather should be related to the activities of each individual and his opportunity to help in developing greater security for himself through eliminating waste of any kind.

Results of action at the top and at other levels as participation expands can be used to indicate to all employees the importance attached to the program. The sincerity of management will be evident and will stimulate the thinking of people down the line throughout the organization. To avoid killing interest, however, we want to be sure that no executive thoughtlessly commits a wasteful act. If it should happen it must be acknowledged and not repeated.

With such interest aroused, the next step is to present the objectives in terms of company needs and problems. We can be specific as to goals, if not actual improvement projects. Better quality and service or lower cost to the customer can mean new plant, new equipment, development of new products, which contribute to the growth, stability, and profit of the company. But most important of all, the accomplishment of such objectives must be related to the individual in terms of better jobs, greater opportunity, pay, security, and recognition. This step may be taken in the first of a series of meetings designed to impart the "know-how" for eliminating waste or solving problems, or it may be accomplished in special meetings of larger groups. In the latter instance, those most interested will make up small groups for the subsequent training sessions.

Departmental Alternative

In some situations it may be difficult or even impossible to interest top management immediately in an overall program of participation with know-how. On the other hand, there may be a division or a major department led by people who are interested in such a program within their part of the organization. Working with that division or department, we can follow much the same procedure outlined for an overall company program. If the departmental program is handled properly, the success within the department will attract the attention of other departments or divisions. As the benefits accumulate, other departments will recognize the desirability of the program and want to get into the act, too. This is the first alternative to an overall company approach, with the same ultimate goal in view.

Staff-to-Worker Contact

In other situations it might not be practical or possible to sell either top management or divisional or departmental management on the idea of general participation with know-how. A staff organization may be charged with the responsibility for developing improvements. Or a department such as accounting or office management may have grown up with a general supervisory responsibility for paperwork procedures and methods. In such a situation, it is far more effective and easier to accomplish results if the staff people will explain to the line people the objectives of their specific studies, how they plan to work, and the techniques to be used. The staff person should admit frankly the need for the line people and should enlist their cooperation. Developing satisfactory improvements and obtaining enthusiastic use of them will be much easier than if the staff person assumes the attitude of an expert and attempts to work out answers by himself.

This is the second alternative to the companywide approach. Fundamentally all three are the same. The difference is in the degree to which we attempt to develop initial participation with training and know-how. With any one of the three approaches, the opening group meeting to generate interest and enthusiasm will pave the way for better results.

Training Follows

When either the companywide or the departmental approach is used, we must be prepared to follow the initial interest-generating meetings with training. With executives this will be more developing an appreciation of the know-how than actual training. At various levels of supervision and with the workers, the training will be detailed and specific techniques will be introduced to fit the needs of the particular groups. It will be carried on with small groups and with every group it should wind up with the complete working out of a project for the solution of a problem.

The fundamental know-how for eliminating waste and developing more effective systems, procedures, and methods is the same whether we are tackling production problems or paperwork problems. When a billing or other paperwork job, for instance, grows beyond the capacity of one person and requires several, knowledge about the various machines or equipment available to handle such a job pays off materially in developing improvements. It is comparable to a knowledge of automatic screw machines and other equipment that would be suitable for handling a lathe job that has similarly grown in volume. The fundamental approach is the same in either case. Only the detailed techniques and equipment will vary with the specific areas or activities studied.

A general understanding of paperwork objectives, problems, and techniques for improving jobs is desirable as a part of the training for several reasons. It is impossible to divorce paperwork from the line activities. In production it is frequently impossible to set up competent controls or paperwork systems without modifying production activities and layout. Very often people seem to

40

like tackling jobs other than their own. Production people like to get into paperwork, which too often has been imposed upon them by others. In imparting know-how we will, therefore, cover the fundamental approach to improvement, together with the techniques used most generally. Supplementing that, there should be an appreciation of the specialized techniques and the services which are available through technicians when required. These specialized techniques include the detailed analysis of operations involving complicated relationships, such as right-and-left-hand or that of the operator to one or more machines; and the use of statistical methods in quality control, work sampling, or in other control accounting. Certainly an appreciation of systems analysis, procedure flow charting, methods for improving the writing process, and the significance of form design, are a must.

Follow-through to Projects

Many companies have generated the all-important initial interest in participation to eliminate waste—and then systematically trained everyone in the organization in techniques. Two mistakes are frequently made with this approach. First, you don't generate enthusiasm by directive. People go through the motions while the heat is on but conveniently forget when the "drive" is over. Second, the training should be only the opening of the door. The group trained should follow through by picking a project and, as a group, working it through to a conclusion. Groups should be set up on a voluntary basis. They should be small, not exceeding six or eight people. The individuals in a group should be of a comparable level within the organization and should be from jobs sufficiently related so that the members will have a common interest in projects or problems.

The first groups particularly should be selected because the individuals have demonstrated interest. If these groups select projects which affect people or functions not covered by the group and that go beyond the scope of the activities covered by the group, representatives of those activities must be included in the group before the study is begun. When these added members have assisted in solving the problem, in most cases, they will ask to be included in the next training group. The participation will expand beyond departmental or divisional areas. And if it grows because people want to "get in," it will be healthy and lasting as contrasted with most "programs." We will achieve a work climate or atmosphere of mutual understanding and confidence. The result will be better relationships, improved production and profit, and more security for everyone.

TWO CASES ILLUSTRATE PRINCIPLES FOR WASTE ELIMINATION

In tackling the problem of paperwork, it is often effective to start with top management forms and reports. As a case in point, the sales analysis prepared monthly for the sales manager of a large company was recently brought to my attention. It listed a breakdown of sales by product, by district, and by salesmen. The tabulation, six lines to the inch, covered almost 100 pages with over 5,000 entries. This detailed report, as we shall see, provides an excellent illustration of one type of waste that has grown fantastically in the guise of better management controls.

In recent years, in "forms control," a great deal of attention has been given to the *forms* in an effort to cut their cost. More recently considerable publicity has been devoted to cutting the cost of *filing* and *storing* records. Both of these approaches have merit, and in large organizations have shown substantial savings. But they frequently miss the major potential for effective savings in large volume. If both are treated as part of an overall balanced program, fine. However, too often the results achieved rather quickly in these areas tend to obscure the possibilities available in the area that comprises the gathering and preparing of the information that goes onto forms and into records, together with the writing, handling, and using of the records and reports.

Many analyses of a wide variety of situations indicate that the cost of the printed forms represents about 5 percent of the total cost of paperwork. The filing and storing of the various records and reports cost another 5 percent of the total paperwork cost. The remaining 90 percent of the cost is involved in the processing of data—writing and handling operations, and distribution and use of the various forms, records, and reports. The significant waste of the sales analysis mentioned was not in form cost or in filing, but in this "90 percent area."

Objectives Are Basic

But before analyzing that waste, let us reexamine some of the objectives which we hope to accomplish through such a report. Several years ago, we defined paperwork in relation to the objectives or end results which we hoped to accomplish through it. In those terms, paperwork is the recording, storing, analysis, and transmission of information for two major purposes: first, to meet government requirements for reports such as income tax, Social Security, unemployment insurance, and others; and second, to help someone do his job better. Work Simplification is the organized application of common sense *by everyone* to eliminate waste—waste of time, energy, space, equipment, materials—waste of any kind. Put the two together and we have an expression of the objectives of *Paperwork Simplification.*

Now let us examine the objectives of the sales manager with the sales analysis. His job is to see that the products are sold in the quantities available, on a basis which will enable the company to make a profit. In the long run, these sales should be made to customers who will be satisfied and will continue to purchase. In addition the members of the sales force must sell in sufficient volume to make an adequate living and provide continuity of the representation. A well-organized company will know its capacity to produce, and the cost of making the product. Idiosyncrasies, such as a highly seasonable market for sales, will be known. Efforts should be made to develop variety in the product line to level such idiosyncrasies and to provide production needs as nearly as possible on a level basis the year around.

43

ANSWERS FROM THE ANALYSIS? In such a company, the sales manager will know the various markets for the products and the potential sales available to his company. He will know the requirements of his various representatives, and plan to enable them to make a satisfactory living. Each representative will have his quota for sales of the various products, related to the potential market which he covers and to his requirements for income.

Under these circumstances, what should general sales managers expect to get from a monthly sales analysis? They should get answers to questions such as these: Are sales up to the schedule planned which will enable us to dispose of the productive capacity? Are the sales being made in the districts and markets as planned? Are the districts and the men making the sales which indicate they are realizing the potential they should, both to develop the company properly and to maintain their own financial status adequately?

In business we know that general business trends will vary and cause deviations from estimates and quotas previously established. We also know that steps can be taken to counteract these effects. But overall, most of the items reported in the more than 5,000 details of the monthly sales analysis will not deviate significantly from the expected.

MECHANIZING FOR MANAGEMENT If a sales manager takes the time to dig out from the 5,000 items those which have deviated significantly, in order that he may take some corrective action, he will spend far more time digging than he will taking action. More likely, because of the tremendous volume of items, the examination will be superficial and will miss many of the significant points. In either event, there is waste—waste of time by the sales manager, or a lack of value derived from the report which represents far more waste than the total cost of accumulating the data and preparing the report.

The report referred to was prepared by punched card equipment. How much better it would be if a percentage of deviations were established as significant and requiring action. The facilities of the automatic equipment could then be used to eliminate

44

those items which did not deviate significantly, leaving in the tabulation only those details which required attention. Where sales by product, district, or salesman were significantly below quota, attention would be called to them. Where sales exceeded quota significantly, value could be derived from finding out the cause and passing the information on to the rest of the sales organization. The time of the general sales manager could be used much more effectively in working on these significant deviations than in trying to locate them.

CONTROL BY EXCEPTION The illustration is typical of much of wasteful paperwork which is costing American business untold dollars. We pay attention to so much minute detail that we don't have time to see the important things. The development of statistical quality control has pointed the way to improvement of tremendous areas of paperwork involved in controls.

In our bank accounts, in paying our people, in paying for goods purchased, and in billing customers, we have to be exact. We must accumulate the detail and do it accurately. But what happens when this approach is carried over into the operation of production, cost, inventory, sales, and other operating controls? We accumulate all the detailed information over a period, frequently a month. At the end of the period, we prepare the reports on what happened. These are available anywhere from one day to a week or perhaps several weeks or more, *after the happening*. It is like locking the stable after the horse has been stolen. We can't do a thing about it. In the extreme situation we might even go broke before we found out why.

In production, for example, we want to know that a bad trend has started *before* the damage is done. To know how much damage was done several weeks ago may be better than nothing, but it is a historical record.

In production, cost, inventory, sales, and other functions, to operate effectively, we must estimate what we expect to do. If we can then apply the practice of "accounting by exception," we can cut our costs tremendously. Through intelligent sampling which can be set up to provide for a reasonable possibility of

45

error, we can spot exceptions in advance and take action at once.

Responsibility Stimulates

In factory production we set effective production standards in terms of time—time per unit of production or number of units per period of time. We also have rather effective measurement in terms of the number of units of product for a given quantity of material used. Since the factors required to convert these units of measurement into dollars are fairly standard, the measurement of activity might just as well be maintained in terms of the original measurement and thus save the waste involved in converting to dollars.

These production measurements are controls; but controls cannot *enforce* the achievement of the results. The only one who can control results is the individual on the job. When proper understanding of the importance of results, not only to the organization but to the person, has been achieved, placing the responsibility with him stimulates the individual and is one of the most effective methods for achieving the goals. Highlighting exceptions or significant deviations enables management to concentrate where the most good can be done.

In spite of the fact that little so-called scientific measurement has been applied to office and clerical work, this basic approach has been applied even to routine clerical jobs on a practical basis. One example illustrates the points. The writing of waybills on a railroad is a high-volume operation. One particular railroad kept track of the number of waybills written at the various points on the road. They knew about how many waybills were written per operator-hour in each office and as an average for the road. Averages in the various offices did not vary too greatly, but in all offices except one, peak periods always required overtime work. In the one office there had been no overtime for a long period, yet the average production per employee-hour was roughly the same as in the other offices.

46

PRODUCTION INCENTIVE   I happened to do some work in the exceptional office and I found that the supervisor, having recognized
the importance of placing responsibility with the people on the
job, had made a deal with his operators. When they had cleaned
up their work, they could leave for the day (though not more
than two hours ahead of normal quitting time) and be paid for a
full day. On the other hand, the deal included their *completing*
the day's work each day. The result was not, as might be supposed, that they cheerfully stayed and earned overtime when the
peak load came along, but rather that they all pitched in and did
a full day's work in order to clean up at the earliest possible
hour. The number of waybills produced per hour paid for—
regardless of whether the operator worked or not—averaged out
as good as, or better than, the other offices. But the unit cost per
waybill typed was all based on standard pay; no overtime was
involved. Other offices paid a premium for a substantial part of
the work. While the measurement used in this instance was not
scientific and was not accurate, it was practical in that it produced the lowest cost results on the entire road. It did not
require a lot of detailed record keeping.

However different, each of these cases illustrates an approach
to the elimination of waste in paperwork. The sales report ex-
emplifies the possibilities for savings through what we might call
accounting by exception or, in other words, through emphasis
upon significant facts rather than on volumes of facts. The way-
billing operation, demonstrating the placing of responsibility
where it belongs, represents one of the most effective incentive
applications that has ever come to my attention. The possibility
for savings through the broad application of both of these approaches is almost unlimited. Any 10 percent saving in this area
of "processing information," which represents 90 percent of paperwork cost, is almost equal to a 100 percent savings in the
forms and the storing areas—which "savings," meaning a total
elimination, are of course out of the question. Without neglecting
savings in the forms or the filing and storing areas, let us concentrate our major attention on the big 90 percent area of cost.

47

Five Steps to Improvement

Parvin S. Titus
Dedicated to
David B. Porter

David B. Porter (1892–1976), a former methods engineer, was a teacher of industrial engineering at New York University. He established the first collegiate laboratory course in motion study, and initiated the NYU Work Simplification Roundtable.

From the time people became interested in analytical thinking, efforts have been made to develop guidelines for solving problems and making improvements. A problem-solving pattern, is required in order to ensure a logical, orderly approach to developing a solution. When presented with a problem, the normal tendency is to propose solutions. Such a problem-solving approach frequently fails to consider many of the pertinent facts, resulting in no solution or a solution which is either unworkable or has a disastrous impact upon associated systems.

Many problem-solving methods have been developed. Dr. Joe McPherson delineated 18 in his book *The People, The Problems and the Problem-Solving Methods* (Midland, MI: Pendell Co., 1967). All of these systems have the objective of moving the problem solver from problem recognition to solution implementation. Some methods are complex, comprising more than 20 steps; others are much simpler. The simplest and most readily applicable is the Five-Step Pattern.

This article has been compiled by Parvin S. Titus from materials developed and used by some of the pioneering teachers of Work Simplification, including A. H. Mogensen, David B. Porter, William R. Mullee, W. A. Hoffman, F. W. Simerson, and others. It is dedicated to the late Professor David B. Porter.

STEP 1: SELECT AND DEFINE THE PROBLEM

All activities are subject to improvement, but for methodical problem solving in an organization, one should select an important problem, such as a job which needs:

> greater productivity
> improved quality
> reduced costs
> better use of materials
> higher equipment output
> improved use of space
> simplified paperwork
> improved working conditions
> reduced fatigue

These things are not always readily apparent. It is easy to walk by the same situation every day without seeing it. Most good improvement programs devote time to teaching how to observe. For many years, supervisory personnel at H. P. Hood and Sons were required to spend one hour per month observing an operation and recording problems.

The best source for discovering an organization's problems is its own people. Ask a person about his problems and he will be glad to tell you. But don't ask if you don't intend to try to solve them. Other sources of ideas are from visitors, suppliers, even competitors.

In looking for improvement prospects it is important to remember that any job consists of three parts:

> *Make ready* the effort and time required to secure and set up the necessary tools, materials, and equipment.
> *Do* the work that accomplishes the objective and adds value to the product.
> *Put away* all the necessary details of unloading, disposal, storage, or clean-up following the *do* stage.

49

The greatest room for improvement lies in eliminating the *do* operation, for if it can be eliminated, the *make-ready* and *put-away* that go with it are automatically eliminated. One must remember that *make-ready* and *put-away* add *cost* but not *value*.

In some cases one may find only an ill-defined feeling that "something is wrong." In such cases detailed analyses may be required. Tools such as work sampling, work distribution charting, or functional analysis are valuable problem finders. When encountering multiple problems in a single area, statistical techniques such as Pareto Analysis may assist in indicating what should be tackled first. In making this decision, don't forget the boss. His priorities must be considered.

After one identifies the problem, it must be defined, preferably in writing. As Charles Kettering said, "A problem well defined is half solved." One must be certain that the problem selected for study is the *cause* of the difficulty, not a *symptom* resulting from a more fundamental problem up or down the productive stream. Everyone concerned should be consulted as the scope of the study is determined (it shouldn't try to cover too much ground) and the benefits to be expected from the improvement are spelled out.

STEP 2: BREAK DOWN AND RECORD THE JOB DETAILS

Once a problem has been defined, one must obtain all the facts about it. These may include cost data, specifications, schedules, samples, production figures, work counts, budgets, and layouts. This is historical data which will shed light on the problem.

Most important is obtaining a detailed description of the operation exactly as it is performed. This cannot be done by sitting at one's desk and thinking about the process. One must observe the operation on site as it is performed, recording the details as they occur. The motion picture camera or videotape recorder provides a complete record which can be analyzed away from the job site. There are also many charting techniques available. Flow process and procedure charts, operator (right- and left-hand) charts, multiple activity or man-machine charts not only record a verbal description of each detail, but employ standard symbols which provide excellent clues for later analysis. Flow diagrams, workplace layouts, and still pictures assist in visualization of the activity.

By recording *all* details in the appropriate manner, one obtains a picture of the subject which everyone can see together. No questions of persons, places, materials, tools, or methods used can cloud discussion on the next step in the process. As Bernard Baruch said, "Every man has a right to his opinion, but no man has a right to be wrong in his facts."

STEP 3: CHALLENGE THE JOB AND EACH DETAIL

This step calls for a look at the job as a whole. What is the purpose of the job? Is it necessary? Does it accomplish the objective? What would result from its elimination? The ultimate goal is elimination of the activity—which would then eliminate the labor of improving superfluous details. There is a significant difference between efficiency and effectiveness. What is the use of doing efficiently what never should be done at all?

If the job is necessary one should then ask:

Where is it being done and *why?* Should it be done elsewhere?

When is it being done and *why?* Should it be done at another time?

Who is doing it and *why?* Should it be done by another person?

How is it being done and *why?* Can it be improved or simplified?

The last question leads to the next phase of this step: challenging the *do* details. Even though the whole job may not be eliminated, the elimination of *do* details internal to the job will result in elimination of the related make-ready and put-away. After the *do* details, the remaining details are questioned in the same manner.

51

Throughout the entire process the questioning procedure follows the same sequence, each question leading to consideration of its own improvement possibilities. *All* suggested changes and improvements should be listed. The open mind is particularly important at this point. Ideas must be permitted to flow freely. Conflicting and controversial proposals may be made; habits and long-standing traditions may be challenged. Any ideas should be welcomed and noted. Critical judgment must be avoided as it inhibits creative participation and will reduce the number of possibilities generated.

STEP 4: DEVELOP A BETTER METHOD

All of the ideas generated are now reviewed to determine which ones individually or in combination with others offer the best solutions. Technical aspects such as cost and timeliness of installation, effects on production, quality, and unit costs must be considered. Also, the human aspects of safety, employee relations, and morale must be explored.

Participation of all those involved is particularly valuable at this point. Use of their knowledge and ideas permits incorporation of features in the new method which can overcome potential objections and lessen resistance to change.

As the proposal takes shape, the team may make assignments to obtain estimates, to run experiments, and to test changes in procedure. The plan must be checked carefully to be certain nothing has been overlooked. A chart of the new method should be prepared. This shows not only how the new method will work, but, in comparison with charts of the old method, demonstrates the advantages of the new.

STEP 5: INSTALL THE IMPROVEMENTS

Prepare a timetable for installation. If all those concerned participated fully during the prior steps, there should be little need to "sell" the proposal. What people help to develop, they will help to install and make work. Pride of ownership and accomplishment overcomes resistance to change, improves morale, and encourages personal growth.

If training in the new method or procedure is required, the charts and diagrams are helpful teaching tools. Purposes and benefits must be thoroughly explained and all questions answered. This process should also be approached with an open mind as even further improvements may result from someone asking "why?"

Once the improvement is in use, one should continue to monitor it to assure proper use, to check for further improvement possibilities, and to document results. A project team can derive little satisfaction without knowing that the improvement meets or exceeds the benefit goals which they established for themselves in Step 1.

Finally, one must give recognition. All documentation and publicity of the change should give full credit to all participants. Proper recognition from one's peers and from top management is a most powerful incentive to further improvement. As in the locker room of the winning team, there's lots of enthusiasm when the whole world knows who won the championship.

What
Every Worker
Wants

Whiting Williams

Whiting Williams (1878−1975), considered by many to be America's first research sociologist, worked in steel mills, coal mines, railroad shops, and oil refineries, trying to gain first-hand knowledge of workers' problems. His classic study What's on the Worker's Mind *was published in 1920. Williams was an early advocate of participative improvement as a requisite of meaningful work.*

The first of my rather unusual efforts to understand the worker started when the president of the steel company for whom I was working called me in one day and said that he and his associates didn't think I was doing a good job of bridging the gap between the mind of management and the minds of the workers. Like anyone else under similar circumstances, I went home and proceeded to walk the floor for a few nights. As a result, I went in and asked him if he would give me a leave of absence for six months for the purpose of living the life of our workers. He gave me permission, but asked the same question that has been asked me ever since by people when they hear of my experiences. Said he: "How will you disguise yourself sufficiently to gain the confidence of the workers?"

I have always had to explain that in the rough labor gangs where I proceeded to live the life of my fellow workmen, all of

Previously unpublished article obtained from A. Fred Kersting, Sr., Dallas, Texas, with permission of Mrs. Whiting Williams.

them accepted me so completely as the ordinary laborer I pretended to be, that it actually hurt my feelings! Only one man pierced my disguise—and he was very intoxicated at the time! He said, "There's something wrong with you, stranger. Either you have been convicted of a serious crime, or you are a victim of some secret sin, or you wouldn't come to work in this god-forsaken town!"

I have to report that what really worried me was the danger of getting too close to the whole situation, especially in various countries abroad. In Russia I was really scared when being interviewed by my fellow coal miners and was suddenly arrested by the secret police who gave me a good workout before they finally released me.

In 1922, *Collier's Weekly* asked me to find out the causes of the great railway shopman's strike. That meant I had to go through the picket lines. I will never forget my reception there. We were being taken in under protection of a policeman, and one picket said, "Hey, has anybody told you about the dynamite that goes off in there? We guys on the outside don't know how many of you dirty scabs get knocked off in there, because the company buries them at night, but it sure does make one hell of a noise!"

During the Depression I ran again into unexpected danger. I had been accepted as a bum in Chicago until I made the mistake of drinking out of a milk bottle a harmless-looking concoction that looked like milk and water. It goes by the name of "smoke," also by the name of "jungle juice." It was a combination of gasoline and denatured alcohol!

What I learned helps explain the miracle of American production—how we have gotten the amazing will to work which now stands us in such good stead.

FEAR, HOPE, AND PRIDE—IMPORTANT WORDS

I took a train in January 1919, to go to Pittsburgh to get a job in the steelworks. I changed my name, put on old clothes, and had

$25 in my pocket, with the expectation that it was up to me to live the life of a jobless man if my $25 gave out. In four hours I ran onto a very important word. That word is fear, the fear of the loss of the job. As long as I live, I will never get over the impression made on me of the universality of that particular fear.

Shortly afterward I learned the importance of a second word in the workman's mind. The word is hope, hope for promotion.

I wish I could claim that I pondered why that fear was so intense and that hope so unquenchable. But I thought I knew. All the professors and the psychologists said they knew all about it. They said the only value in the worker's mind was money, that the fear was only fear for the loss of income, that the hope was only the hope for a larger income.

I had plenty of time to ponder that question, and the longer I pondered the less adequate that explanation appeared to be. To make a long story short, there is a third word that goes with fear and hope in the workman's mind. That word is pride. I believe that pride represents the satisfaction of the two deepest, strongest, most useful of hankerings. Hankering number one is for our own self-respect, the right to believe that we individually represent certain values in the scheme of things—that we are worthwhile, important, "somebody." If you think that is an easy satisfaction to enjoy, let me say, on the contrary, the enjoyment of that particular satisfaction represents just about the hardest job that you or I or anyone knows about, for the reason that I have yet to see a human being of any sort who is as sure of his or her right to believe in his or her importance as he or she would like to be.

When I say that, I will gamble that half of you will say, "You are right," but half of you will say "You are wrong." But none of us are all the time as sure of ourselves as we would like to be. Whether we are drunk or sober, young or old, male or female, sane or insane, all of us are everlastingly trying to fight off the feeling of having to think of ourselves as a human zero of insignificance and unimportance.

That leads to hankering number two, the hankering we all have for the confirmation of our right to enjoy our self-respect which comes to us from sources outside ourselves, in the form of recognition, esteem, honor.

I recommend, therefore, as most helpful to understanding the worker's mind, these fundamentals.

First, that today the saving of our physical skin has become infinitely less important as a factor in our human relations than the saving of our social "face." This is so dependent upon our right to think well of ourselves and the attention we get, that our "face" is very easily hurt by some slur, some look of the eye, or other small slight.

Secondly, that whereas today at least two-thirds of the human race are bothered by hunger, here in America our hunger for food has become infinitely less important than hunger for attention, recognition, understanding. If you want to annoy any human being, all you have to do is ignore him or her!

Third, that our hunger finds its chief and surest satisfaction in connection with our jobs, our work. I think I can claim rather varied contacts. To learn about people, I have associated with bums and with workers here and abroad, and I have sat with captains of industry in London, Paris, Berlin, Chicago, and New York. I give you my word: Whether they were bums, board chairmen, or in-betweens, they are all just about equally less sure of themselves than they would like to be, all about equally as hungry to maintain "face," to have a word of approval.

But here is the point. Whether they were at the bottom or the top of the ladder, every blessed one of them gave me as final, incontrovertible proof of his right to believe in himself the same certificate: "This is my job; this is the kind of service I give my fellow men; this is the kind of equipment I make useful to my fellow citizens. On the basis of that I demand a certain amount of attention."

THE JOB—A MEASUREMENT OF USEFULNESS

I found, therefore, that the job serves as an amazingly useful scale for measuring the distance we have achieved up from the useless zero. Thus, I finally got a job as a laborer in the cinder-pit of a steel plant. Three weeks later the boss asked me about going into the millwright gang. I supposed only the money would be of interest to the ordinary worker. So when he told me I would get only two cents more an hour I thought it wasn't important. An hour later I had the new tools in my hand, and when I came by old companions I made a sensation. Every blessed one of them greeted me: "Hey! No more pick and shovel for you! My God, you are one lucky son-of-a-gun!"

That was the first of a series of experiences that taught me that to every worker his job represents a rung upon a ladder indicating his comparative importance, establishing his position as a man among his fellow citizens outside the job. Every rung represents a distance, established partly by the amount of money but also by the skill and the training required. Thousands of details are involved. A tool designer feels he has a right to consider himself a more important person and citizen than the tool operator, because of his job. Likewise the tool operator considers himself more important than the sweeper. Everywhere it's like that.

We have today a serious problem just because the whole trend of these modern times, with which I don't agree, is to lesson the differential between the skilled man and the unskilled by raising the unskilled.

The point is that when we give honor and recognition to the man at the top of the ladder, anyone from the bottom up has the right to consider himself worthwhile because his job makes him essential to the man at the top.

When I became an assistant repairman in a mine in Wales, I was way down below the lowest level, a thousand feet down. . . . Evan Pugh, the repairman, and I would be hoping for a message to do our stuff. Then one of the miners would come in and say, "Evan, you better come quick before the pit falls in!" Half an hour afterward we would realize that only after we had done that repair job could the whole mine start working again. Then Evan would say to me, "It's very plain to see they can't run their bloody mine without you and me!"

There is nothing that can compare with a man's job for helping him believe in himself. Everywhere I have gone, I have found the same thing. The reason we have such a grand, responsible bunch of locomotive engineers is because they get the kowtowing of all their associates and companions because they have gone from the bottom of the ladder up to the top. What we overlook is that the fireman is likely to say, as one of them once said to me as I rode with him: "You see, the engineer takes himself very seriously. I ain't saying nothin', but let me tell you, Mr. Engineer don't get his engine very far unless he gets his power from me!"

EVERYBODY'S JOB IS IMPORTANT TO HIM

You can't think of anybody whose job doesn't seem to him important. One time I unintentionally insulted the International Secretary of the Hobo Union because I thought he was a tramp. He said, "We 'boes are migratory workers, itinerant laborers; if we don't go to the right part of the country at the right time, millions of dollars' worth of crops go to hell. So we take the train. A tramp only walks for a job. A bum is a guy that neither rides nor walks nor works. He's no good." . . .

Nobody can be sure of the loyalty of his workers unless he understands this absolutely fundamental fact. Of course, a job puts money in a man's pocket, but most important, it also puts self-respect and self-belief in the bottom of his heart. If you miss that, you miss everything!

It is this tie-up of soul and body represented by the job that explains the fear I mentioned earlier. That fear, in turn, explains many of the peculiarities of workers. It "justifies" unions, limitation of output, and so on. It also explains the worker's hope for promotion. Besides an increase in income, this means a larger distance away from that dreadful zero at the bottom.

This tie-up also means that every single one of us would like to take pride in our work. If we can't take pride in our jobs, we can't take pride in ourselves, and then you might as well seek our body at the bottom of the river.

That tie-up also explains why your feelings, my feelings, every worker's feelings, can be hurt more easily during the hours of our job than any other of the day. Your spouses may say you are touchy enough when you come home, but it doesn't compare with your touchiness during the hours of your job. It also explains why big issues come from management's failure to take care of some little annoyance that hurts people's feelings.

In my opinion, many labor leaders understand these fundamentals better than employers, particularly the wish of their members to feel important, if not in their work, then in a strike. They also realize the importance of little things. . . . One reason why the big unions have done as much as they have is because they first send out investigators who bring back all the gripes, big and little. They send out their organizers to tell every member of that industry, "If you sign on the dotted line, you will never again be bothered by any of these troubles."

I have found this importance of the job everywhere, but nowhere to the extent as here in the United States. We have outproduced the rest of the world for the reason that we have harnessed the performance of useful service to those two hankerings. We have said to our youngsters, "If you would like to grow up into a worthy citizen with the confirmation and esteem of your fellows, all you need to do is climb that ladder of the job!" . . .

Today I am worried because that system of respectability and honor based upon work which has made us great is now under serious threat. You have the greatest of all opportunities to help save our system of making respectability and honor depend upon work. For if I am right about the importance of fear, hope, and pride, then, as employers, you have a greater opportunity than anybody else, first, to lessen fear; secondly, to justify hope; and most important and difficult, to build pride in your workers—pride of their skill, pride of their craft, pride of their company, pride of their industry. Pride is the key to their performance.

VALUE OF PERSONAL CONTACTS

Here are a few of the tools which you can use for building pride. The simplest and one of the most effective tools is making sure that you are utilizing to the full your opportunity for personal contacts. I have been a fan about what can be done by personal contact ever since I got a job in the mines in Germany's Saar Valley. I was told the German miners were going to murder the French engineers who were put over them by the League of Nations. But to my surprise they spoke well of these officers.

In explanation, the engineers said, "We are taught in our mining schools always to keep in close touch with our miners. Every day we talk to a few of them face to face till in a month we contact all of them." Sure enough, I'd be loading coal and along would come the French engineer-manager. He would ask us, "How are you getting along? Have you got good tools? Is the ventilation all right?" Then after talking with us about the cost of living, and so on, he would say, "We will see you again next month."

Most amazed, the Germans would exclaim, "We have been taught to hate every Frenchman, yet they treat us better than we have ever been treated before."

So I say today, American industry is in danger of depending too much on mass arrangements, mass programs. But if you leave out personal contacts, those programs won't work. Our heavy dependence on these big mass plans in industry isn't much more silly than if some husband were to say that he and his wife, in order to avoid divorce, were going to sign a contract that would cover every problem. So if he was blown up by his wife on a Tuesday morning he could point to page so-and-so and say, "See, this clause proves you're wrong!" There is no substitute for personal contact for learning the worker's fears, hopes, and prides.

ANSWERING THE WHY'S

The second tool is better communications, fuller explanation of *why* the new machine or the new method. You can't overdo it. Whether you are a mother in the home or a boss in the factory, when you ask me to do so-and-so "because I tell you" you are destroying my face, my belief in myself. I wish I could put upon the desk of every executive and manager a sign saying, "Explain. Explain. If you can't explain, explain why you can't explain."

The next tool I recommend is the freer use of the pat on the back, when deserved. Mind you, I underline the word "deserved," because if you want to lose the respect of a good craftsman, you need only praise as good a job which he as a craftsman knows is lousy. I have had vice-presidents of some of the biggest corporations in America almost weep on my shoulder because they couldn't get from their president one single word to enable them to know where they stood. They would give their right arm to have a report back from the president with two words, "Very good," instead of just two initials.

A manager told me one time in a plant in Cleveland that he called in a foreman and told him that the vice-president had asked if he could lend him for a couple of weeks to another plant. "I told him I couldn't spare him because he was too useful to me." Result? Big Jim, the foreman, said with tears in his eyes, "I have wondered all these years if you thought I was any damn good. That's the best news ever!" . . .

When you give a man a job in your plant you give him something infinitely more important than a chance to make a living. You determine the conditions of his whole life. If he can feel, with your help, the right to consider himself worthwhile, as playing a worthy part in the protection and maintenance of America, then you have built that man into a happy human being in the way that no other human being of any sort can do as well as you, his employer.

All this has a more important meaning today than ever before, because we are in a war of "isms"—different ideas of human nature and motivation. The best statement I have seen of our American idea was given by Fosdick. He says, "The essence of Americanism and of democracy is to attribute to ordinary human beings extraordinary possibilities."

We Americans don't follow the line of least resistance. We have no respect for a leader who asks so little of us that we can't think better of ourselves than we could before. We hate a leader who takes all the credit and the glory and gives us nothing but the money. But we gladly go through hell for the leader who asks the impossible of us—provided that, when we give it, he shares with us the right to think better of ourselves in the measure of our effort!

All this means, finally, is that you can't do your best for yourself, for your workers, or for your country, unless you have in mind the limitless possibilities that are placed inside of us by those two hankerings. Rather than fall down and be considered unworthy, we are glad to pay the price of life itself. . . . What has made us great and what will continue to make us great is our willingness to give honor and recognition to a man in proportion to the usefulness of his service.

Old Evan Pugh used to tell me about an under-manager that he worked for who was very hard-boiled—until he studied human nature as captain of a company on the western front during World War I. There he learned about the possibilities of human nature. So when he came back to his old job he put into operation a different way of handling men. One night Old Evan reported: "Yesterday the under-manager down in the pit said to me, 'That was a first-class job you've done.' " And I said to him, "Mr. Under-manager, in forty-three years of workin' in this pit—in forty-three years—that was the first time that any company man said to me a kindly word about my job.' " Then he continued: "Every man knows that for a kindly word, he'll work his guts out—that no dog behaves well for the man with a whip. And every man of sensibility knows that for him, the whip of the tongue and the lash of the lip are worse than any whip on any dog! Every man must have a chance here on the job to show himself a man!"

My belief, therefore, is that we may come through just because, as I have gone among the other nations, I have found this one thing is true of you and me as Americans—namely, that every one of us would love to have it said of us what the writer in Ecclesiasticus [Apocrypha] said of the ancient artisans and craftsmen:

All these have put their trust in their hands, And each becometh wise in his own works. Yea, though they be not sought for in the council of the people, Nor be exalted in the assembly; And be not found amongst them that utter dark sayings; Yet without these shall not a city be inhabited, Nor shall men sojourn or walk up and down therein. For these maintain the fabric of the world. And in the handiwork of their craft is their prayer.

So long as your employers help make sure that our prayer remains there in the work of our hands and our hearts and our heads, the future of America is safe; but with the utmost seriousness may I say, only so long.

I give you four words as helpful to this understanding of the worker and the gaining of his cooperation. Those four words are: Listen, Explain, Respect, Appreciate!

Improvement Must Be Managed

Herbert F. Goodwin

Herbert F. Goodwin is senior lecturer at MIT's Sloan School of Management. He is also a lecturer, an author, and a consultant to numerous industrial improvement programs.

The greatest danger to management thinking in this age of specialization is obsolescence. Improvement is accelerating everywhere at such a rate that we need a planned program to meet the threat. Each of us, as well as the companies with which we are associated, must improve more rapidly just to stay even. If we are to achieve this objective and move out in front, we must deliberately manage the process.

It has been my privilege to address this conference on two previous occasions. Twice I have issued a warning and a challenge that we must keep up with the rate of change. Twice I have summarized how my personal thinking has shifted with the times and have urged you to review your own experiences in the light of current events. I am flattered to be invited back for the third time and blithely ignore the inference of failure that the adage would attribute to the preceding efforts.

To some of you, my remarks will be informative and provocative and, I hope, will leave you stimulated to broaden your own

Proceedings of the 19th Annual Conference of the American Institute of Industrial Engineers, May 1968. Republished from *The Journal of Industrial Engineering,* May 1968. Copyright © 1968 by the American Institute of Industrial Engineers, Inc., Norcross, Ga. 30092.

thinking within a simple effective framework of planned improvement activity. To others, these remarks will draw resonant smiles of experience as comments are made on fundamental concepts which time has all too slowly etched deep into the minds of successful industrial engineers and professional managers who may pick up just one new idea to add strength to their professional efforts. To a few, but still too many, these same remarks will be interpreted as critical and will be dismissed with little consideration until this small minority learns the hard way or switches its endeavor, never knowing why its efforts were so ineffective.

PROGRESS IS SLOW

There has been progress. It just has not been fast enough or on as broad a front as it could have been or should now be. To a great extent this is our own fault. It is too easy to get carried away by our personal enthusiasm for one particular area of interest and possibly lose sight of the ultimate objective. It seems quite evident that the same mistakes are naively being made over and over by well-meaning newcomers and a few bull-headed old-timers. Good executives have precious little time for those who lose themselves in their own special interest or who repeat costly errors, even though the errors were first made by someone else years ago.

The unfortunate aspect of this situation is that these flagrant errors in our field are well documented, but many of us have neglected to read our history lessons. Others, endowed with abundant ability in mathematics and enchanted with the computer, have completely ignored the fundamental tools of industrial engineering and have passed over these same lessons with an attitude that seems to indicate that such things are at too low a level for their talents. As a consequence, we find time studies still being made with hidden devices and computerized answers which are thrust upon managers by experts of the black box who still assume that their findings will be used with blind faith, whether by a lathe operator, a shipping-room foreman, or a regional vice-president of sales.

66

Many well-meaning modern efficiency experts of the "let me tell you how to do it" set are still running the same gamut as their counterparts of 40 years ago who spent 90 percent of their time trying to get people to use their ideas and only 10 percent of their time thinking up those ideas. Many of these modern-day versions fail to realize what is happening when their popularity is something less than they feel is their due.

A Hard Look at Ourselves First

If we would spearhead the improvement effort throughout our companies we must concentrate attention on ourselves first. . . . It is not enough to be able to apply our industrial engineering techniques to find improved methods or to develop better rules for decision-making. The methods must be used and the decisions made with enthusiastic vigor by the people responsible for the end results. Thus, the question that continually must be posed and answered at the policy level is, "Who can get this job done most effectively?"

Achievement of our own personal objectives is the byproduct of our ability to get results through and with other people. Results will depend mostly on our interpersonal relations. Few of us, if any, can say we have never messed up a project because we forgot the people involved. My own sad experiences in this regard are most vivid in my memory. The trouble is that we rarely realize how often or when our thoughtlessness violates the fundamentals of good human relations. We need to work constantly at the problem of interpersonal relations since it transcends all of our activities.

Who Is Our Unknown Competitor?

Recently, I asked this question of the president of a large appliance company. My query disturbed him a bit because he felt certain that he knew all of his competitors and named them. After an hour's discussion we decided that our unknown competitor was: "Anyone else with an idea that we did not have and that could be used in our job or our business." These unknown competitors ranged from the young men in the technical institutions and colleges throughout the country, who walk around with stars in their eyes and do not know what cannot be done, to the man in our own field who has never given us trouble before but who now, with a new product, a new idea, or a new concept of management, emerges as a major threat to our well-being.

The same question may well be asked here. Who is our unknown competitor? Who are the men, young or old, with different approaches who are saying, "We can do it better," and getting the chance to try? It is not hard to identify a few of them.

Financial and accounting specialists are uniquely in possession of the facts as they make their regular audits and reports. More and more they are identifying problem areas, then getting the assignments to set up the procedures and controls for implementing the needed improvements. The banks which are also in the same position are joining them and, in addition, often want a say in the way funds are used.

The social and behavioral scientists are talking more and more of productivity as they concentrate on motivation and the satisfiers of Douglas McGregor's Theory Y.[1] Results are astounding some executives as they wonder about the effectiveness of their traditional industrial engineering approach. Staff specialists in this area are appearing on numerous organization charts and are having a substantial impact on the process of implementing change. Some are also taking the initiative in designing the changes and, in their turn, often forget the human relations involved.

At an executive gathering recently, I heard a minister say that he felt the call to help industry improve its productivity as a spiritual need of society. He was busily engaged in this effort and had figures to show his effectiveness. He is currently a popular speaker at management conferences with a full calendar.

---

[1] See Douglas McGregor, *The Human Side of Enterprise* (New York: McGraw-Hill, 1960.)

There are computer specialists, mathematicians, statisticians, and many others, often with little or no management experience, who are sending the message, "I can do it better," and they are getting an ear.

The Numbers Game

These new faces, in this age of specialization and mounting cost reduction pressures of the profit squeeze, have resulted in a curious fragmentation of the improvement effort in many companies. Separate programs, all with much the same objective, each headed by its own group of specialists or coordinators, have been set up under the aegis of narrow functional groups with an independent mandate for action.

Top management has often supported these groups on a "lip service only" basis to "get the monkey off their backs" while they do more important things. Such leadership exhibits little more than superficial knowledge of the interrelationships of each program with the others, their impact on the routine responsibilities of running the shop, or the time demands on the management personnel affected.

It is only natural that everyone else in the organization should reflect the same attitude as the executives and try to get the monkey off their backs so that they too can get on to more important things. Such situations have spawned a colossal "numbers game" with arbitrary quotas for projects completed, people participating, [and] dollars or man-hours saved. The contest becomes one of manipulating the numbers under pressure of meeting deadlines in such a way as still to have some time to get the regular work done. This kind of numbers game is rarely looked on with enthusiasm by those who must play it.

Unhealthy Symptoms

Typical symptoms of an unhealthy situation are duplications in reporting, the holding back of activities to be sure of meeting next month's quotas, and the trumping up of insignificant projects just to list them or their participants on a progress report. Since most of these fragmented programs are oriented [toward] one particular technique, the specialists or coordinators find themselves fighting for the credit to justify their existence. Competition between groups becomes a personal struggle that degenerates into petty politics.

It is only natural that the line manager rebels against reporting his activities through a staff specialist, particularly when he considers improvement as a part of his job which he would do anyway.

A Single Effective Program

Enlightened management realizes that improvement is one of its prime functions and as such must be managed. When all improvement activity is consolidated into one coordinated program under the direction of the top executives, the results of which are measured by the profitable growth of the company, and everyone identifies his own progress with that of the company, we have an entirely different environment. Total effectiveness of the whole organization emerges as the ultimate objective.

Things begin to fall into place when the emphasis in the improvement effort shifts from training programs and the numbers game to getting things done. "Learn by doing" becomes the method of teaching as the manager at all levels assumes his proper leadership role and accepts the responsibilities of managing improvement in his own area of accountability. Today's real problems become the vehicle for developing the managerial effectiveness of those in his charge. Staff specialists become indispensable resource reservoirs rather than unwanted experts as their specialized knowledge is recognized as a necessity. A new kind of rapport develops into mutual confidence and respect. Problems rapidly become opportunities as the whole task grows into a team effort. The competitive urge is aligned for everyone in a single direction of a common objective as managers seek even more than their share of staff help which is charged to them as part of their budget.

70

IMPROVEMENT MANAGEMENT[2]

An idea does not care who has it. We just have to have the wisdom and the humility to use a good one no matter where it comes from—whether it comes from our boss, our colleagues, our competitors, the people who work with us, or our wives and families. It has often been said that if we steal one idea, it is plagiarism; but if we steal two ideas, it is research. Figure 1 summarily brings together the conglomeration of ideas which I have "researched" during a career of endeavor to help improve the way we improve. The essence of the chart is not just the ideas but, in particular, the interrelationships between them which may open new doors of opportunity and lead us to achieve our goals and objectives more effectively—both company and personal.

Judgment and Local Knowledge

The requirement of adding good judgment and local knowledge to the wisdom of experience was brought home most vividly the first time my son went deer hunting with me. He was, naturally, quite perturbed and a bit confused with the logic of some of our local laws when he was required to pass an examination on handling a rifle as a prerequisite to receiving a license. We were planning to hunt with bows and arrows. He passed the rifle test.

A week before the opening day he had shown no initiative to do any planning or to research the literature. A prod from his father resulted in his nose becoming deeply buried in the bookshelf in my study set aside for such reference material. He found the history books on the experiences of other hunters most interesting and accepted my challenge that he should run the hunt on Saturday. When we awoke on the big day it was pouring rain, and I was pleased that his enthusiasm was not dampened as we

---

[2] Leo B. Moore and Herbert Goodwin of the MIT School of Industrial Management have coined the term "improvement management" to describe a way of gaining some of the benefits of scientific management without producing resistance to change.

71

Figure I. Improvement management.

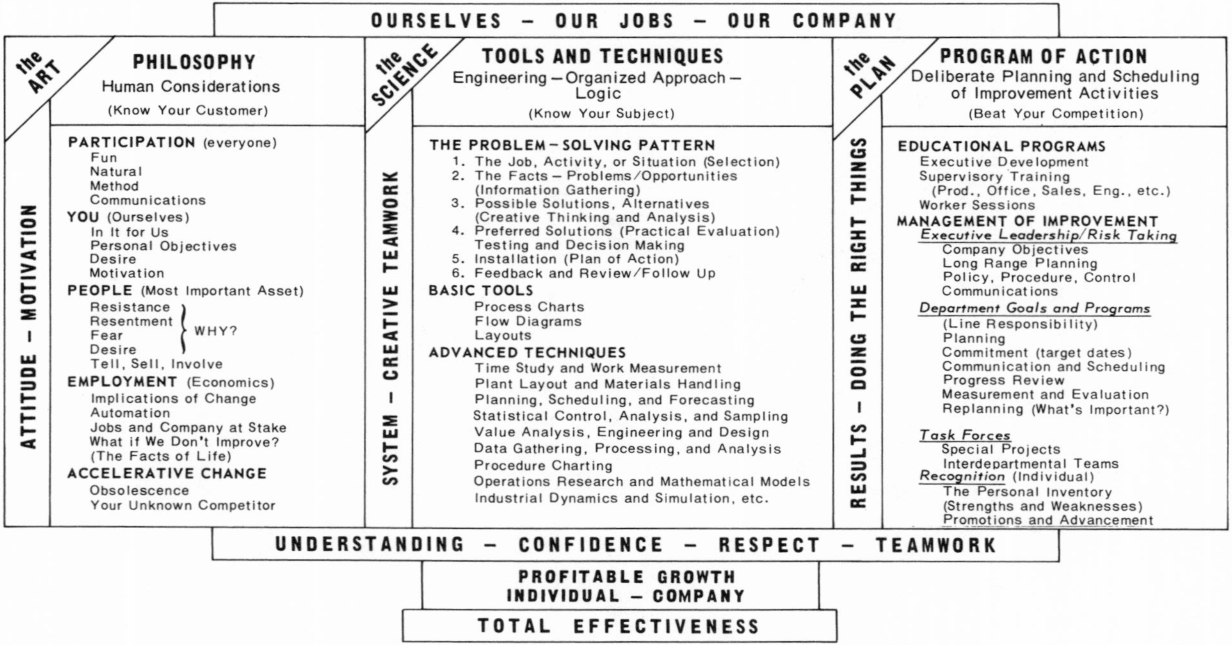

OURSELVES – OUR JOBS – OUR COMPANY

the ART

ATTITUDE – MOTIVATION

PHILOSOPHY
Human Considerations
(Know Your Customer)

PARTICIPATION (everyone)
- Fun
- Natural
- Method
- Communications

YOU (Ourselves)
- In It for Us
- Personal Objectives
- Desire
- Motivation

PEOPLE (Most Important Asset)
- Resistance
- Resentment } WHY?
- Fear
- Desire
- Tell, Sell, Involve

EMPLOYMENT (Economics)
- Implications of Change
- Automation
- Jobs and Company at Stake
- What if We Don't Improve?
  (The Facts of Life)

ACCELERATIVE CHANGE
- Obsolescence
- Your Unknown Competitor

the SCIENCE

SYSTEM – CREATIVE TEAMWORK

TOOLS AND TECHNIQUES
Engineering – Organized Approach –
Logic
(Know Your Subject)

THE PROBLEM–SOLVING PATTERN
1. The Job, Activity, or Situation (Selection)
2. The Facts – Problems/Opportunities
   (Information Gathering)
3. Possible Solutions, Alternatives
   (Creative Thinking and Analysis)
4. Preferred Solutions (Practical Evaluation)
   Testing and Decision Making
5. Installation (Plan of Action)
6. Feedback and Review/Follow Up

BASIC TOOLS
- Process Charts
- Flow Diagrams
- Layouts

ADVANCED TECHNIQUES
- Time Study and Work Measurement
- Plant Layout and Materials Handling
- Planning, Scheduling, and Forecasting
- Statistical Control, Analysis, and Sampling
- Value Analysis, Engineering and Design
- Data Gathering, Processing, and Analysis
- Procedure Charting
- Operations Research and Mathematical Models
- Industrial Dynamics and Simulation, etc.

the PLAN

RESULTS – DOING THE RIGHT THINGS

PROGRAM OF ACTION
Deliberate Planning and Scheduling
of Improvement Activities
(Beat Your Competition)

EDUCATIONAL PROGRAMS
- Executive Development
- Supervisory Training
  (Prod., Office, Sales, Eng., etc.)
- Worker Sessions

MANAGEMENT OF IMPROVEMENT
Executive Leadership/Risk Taking
- Company Objectives
- Long Range Planning
- Policy, Procedure, Control
- Communications

Department Goals and Programs
(Line Responsibility)
- Planning
- Commitment (target dates)
- Communication and Scheduling
- Progress Review
- Measurement and Evaluation
- Replanning (What's Important?)

Task Forces
- Special Projects
- Interdepartmental Teams

Recognition (Individual)
- The Personal Inventory
  (Strengths and Weaknesses)
- Promotions and Advancement

TEAMWORK

UNDERSTANDING – CONFIDENCE – RESPECT

PROFITABLE GROWTH
INDIVIDUAL – COMPANY

TOTAL EFFECTIVENESS

set out at dawn. It was evident that he had done his homework well when he cautioned me never to raise my voice above a whisper and communicate, if at all possible, with sign language while in the woods.

We hunted the low cover in the hour or two after dawn and then worked our way up onto the hardwood ridge which adjoins our New Hampshire summer property without seeing hide nor hair of a deer or any fresh signs. My son motioned me to join him in a conference which I did with high hopes that we might return home for a siesta and dry out for a while.

The whispered conversation went something like this. Son: "No deer." Dad: "That's right. No deer." Son: "I wonder where they are." Dad: "So do I. What do you think?" Son: "Well, I don't know where they are, but I do know if I were a deer I wouldn't be out here in the open getting soaking wet." Dad: "Where would you be?" Son: "Well, I think I'd be over in that ravine half way down the other side of the ridge where those big hemlocks blew down last spring. I stayed dry under one of them for two hours during a heavy shower when I was caught there last summer." Dad: "Let's go and see."

We did, they had, and he got his first shot!

The big lesson is quite clear. He got results because he started with the wisdom of his predecessors and the experience of others as a base; he added his own judgment and knowledge of local conditions to the particular situation in which he found himself and then did the right thing to achieve the desired result.

Like each hunting ground, every business enterprise is different. Local conditions have an overwhelming influence on the outcome of our efforts. The ideas summarily outlined in Figure 1 can be useful as a basic framework within which we may find a starting point. If our efforts to improve are to be effective, we must all add our own judgment and local knowledge to the case at hand and develop our own plans of action.

As we glance at the chart let us take a mental inventory of our own situation and think ahead to the key question of what may be our most important project: "How can we improve the way we improve?"

73

Become People-Oriented

A new awareness of the human considerations is permeating management thinking everywhere. Evidence, documented for us by men like Schell, Williams, McGregor, Likert, and Myers, is overwhelming. People are our most important asset, and their attitudes and motivational drives are a major factor in any successful business.

Most of our human problems seem to be associated with the people who resist our ideas or whom we cannot get to do things the way, or as well as, we want them to. In my opinion, we spend far too much time worrying about the attitudes and motivations of other people and not enough about our own. A good place to start is with ourselves. Consider the competitive edge if everyone in a company improved his own effectiveness by just 10 percent. This is not an unreasonable figure and should be quite easily attainable, since most of us would agree that the actual company utilization of our own potential would be considerably below 90 percent. I have taken the trouble to ask numerous groups at all levels to record their estimate of this percentage as it applies to them and the average has been precious little above 50 percent. I hasten to add that the average changes little whether it be the top executives, a group of engineers, supervisors, or hourly production workers.

The difference between the percentage we feel is now being utilized and 100 percent might be called our opportunity quotient, but it often becomes our frustration factor when we do not get the chance to do anything about it.

Participation—A Motivator

There are few of us who feel that we are given as great an opportunity to participate as we should like. May I suggest that our own chances may come more often if we get in the habit of asking for the participation of those who are in our charge and who can help us.

Whiting Williams says, "We are all driven by the same two

deep-down hankerings. One of these, the first and foremost, is for our self-respect—the right to believe in ourselves . . . to consider ourselves a worthwhile somebody."[3]

The late Professor Erwin H. Schell of MIT said, "Before our very eyes are legions of experienced *work managers* who, if given proper recognition as authentic parts of the management team, will profit greatly from increased self-respect and contribute immensely to the welfare and the progress of their industry."[4]

The greatest compliment you can pay a man, the surest confirmation of his personal worth you can provide, is to ask his advice and help. Everyone has ideas that are worthwhile and we all want to contribute these ideas and will do so if given the chance.

Sensitivity to Reality

Attitudes change quickly and sometimes most unexpectedly. It is next to impossible to be alert to every change, but we certainly can improve our batting average by being more sensitive to the conditions which affect these attitudes.

I recall a recent incident when a colleague of mine and I literally dropped in on the Cleveland Municipal Stadium as we were flying by in the hope of seeing the Red Sox put another one in their win column at the expense of the Indians. The runway at the Lakefront Airport at Cleveland ends practically against the leftfield bleacher wall and we had a few hours to spare so we took advantage of the situation. It was bat day and close to 15,000 youngsters had taken their dads to the game or found one at the gate. We sat just back of third base and a little toward left field, completely surrounded by bat-wielding young men who were naturally partial to the Indians.

It was a close game and the Sox were behind as they came to

[3]Whiting Williams, *America's Mainspring and the Great Society* (New York: Frederick Fell, Inc., 1967), p. 71.
[4]Herbert F. Goodwin and Leo B. Moore, *Management Thought and Action in the Words of Erwin H. Schell* (Cambridge, Mass.: MIT Press, 1967), p. 127.

bat in the ninth. The first batter up was Rico Petrocelli and he lined the first ball pitched foul right at us. I managed to duck, but my more agile colleague sitting at my left reached up and caught the ball with one hand. Thirty-five thousand people roared their approval of such a fielding gem and my friend waved the ball in his hand in pleased response as the TV cameras, no doubt, turned our way with a zoom. At this moment, two or three dozen youngsters reached out their hands for the ball and one nearly succeeded in snatching it from the upstretched arm of my colleague, but he held on. Promptly, most, if not all, of the 35,000 cheers became boos. There was a time when I thought we were not going to make it back to the plane without the ball being forcibly taken away from us. How quickly the attitude changed, and without the least consideration that my colleague had a young son of his own at home to whom he wanted to give the ball. Incidentally, to make matters worse, the Red Sox lost.

Sometimes we do an excellent job, but through a quirk of circumstances the attitudes shift in spite of the facts and we come out losers. If we work at it, though, do not repeat mistakes, and are sensitive to the changing conditions, we will most surely find that our batting average continues to rise.

Sincerity versus Manipulation

A sure way to lose respect is to try to manipulate people into thinking our idea is theirs. The "tell them" approach of the authoritarian is held in low regard, but the insincerity of the manipulator who tries to "sell" his own ideas by subterfuge rarely meets with anything but stiffening resistance. None of us likes to be "taken in" or treated as a fool, and we resent those who try.

People do not resist change as much as they do the methods of change. Actually, it can be shown with a high degree of certainty that most of us like to change and we are particularly enthusiastic about changing when we are involved in developing the innovation. We must remember that the inference of all change is criticism of things as they are and none of us likes criticism, be it constructive or otherwise. On the other hand, if everyone associated with a given activity is involved in the efforts to improve it and the managerial leader sincerely recognizes that his people can and do have ideas to contribute to the total effort, the negative aspects of the implied criticism disappear within the positive satisfiers of recognition through involvement.

Job Security

In spite of our affluence, a universal fear of unemployment as a result of technological advances lingers as a barrier to innovation. As we delve into methods of dealing with specific situations, we soon realize that there is no universal solution to this problem. Yet a solution we must find in each case if we are to progress at anywhere near our potential.

Growth is, perhaps, the ideal answer for the long range, while better forecasting and smoothing of the employment cycle can help in the short run. Open discussions of the relationship of the turnover rate to the improvement rate in any company start most people on the way to better understanding of the situation. The facts of life are clear. If we do not make the new products that replace our old ones, someone else will. Few viable companies are making the same products they did just a few years ago. Constant retraining of people in all areas is a must; and participation at all levels in a mutual effort to cope with the local problem communicates a sincere concern on the part of management and leads to a broader understanding. It readily becomes apparent that there will be few jobs for anyone if our competitor takes over.

People who identify themselves with the company as members of a team and see their own future enhanced by its profitable growth are more likely to accept their responsibility for joining the improvement program. As understanding develops, attitudes change and positive motivation grows.

Creative Teamwork

The systematic organized approach of the "scientific method" came into prominence in the early part of this century. Taylor, Gilbreth, and Gantt were the three pioneers of that era who gave us the fundamental tools and techniques for developing improvements upon which most of management science is based today. Countless other tools have been developed and with the coming of the computer, the evolution of new and more sophisticated techniques has accelerated to the point where it is almost an explosion.

Since it has become virtually impossible for managers or engineers alike to be knowledgeable and skilled to a high level of proficiency in all or even a major portion of these techniques, it is increasingly obvious that specialists are here to stay. The wise leader uses all of the available tools and all of his people to generate improvements and implement the results. He succeeds because of the way he goes at it—the way he manages the process. His approach stands out in dramatic contrast to that of the early experts and authoritarians of a fast disappearing era. He is the master of the situation because he knows his workers and is willing to face the new problems that arise as a result of his efforts to involve them.

The effective innovator puts people and techniques together in a new and powerful pattern of progress that is constantly being redesigned by those who participate in its use. It is this constant improvement of the methods of innovation by those using them that adds new strength across the board.

The vehicle for the application of creative teamwork is the problem-solving pattern. This is the framework within which all the specialized tools and techniques may be systematically utilized to identify opportunities, gather facts, devise better alternatives, make decisions, plan implementations, and measure results. When everyone knows this pattern, and the basic tools from which the more sophisticated techniques are developed, and understands the relationships between them, they all take on new significance. The specialist is no longer suspect as people begin to see their own responsibilities in a new perspective.

Mutual confidence and respect grow into a new kind of understanding which fosters teamwork. Those with the direct responsibility for results begin to ask more often for the help of the staff specialists as the concept of a common goal comes more sharply into focus. The mysticism of the "black box" disappears as the more sophisticated techniques become natural extensions of the simple basic tools which are more readily understood by all. Everyone begins to realize that all of the tools, including those as yet not invented, must be combined with people if we are to get the best results.

We can be highly motivated, have the most positive of attitudes, and perform our assignment with the highest level of enthusiasm, using the best and most appropriate techniques, but if we expend our energies doing the wrong things, we become frustrated, the results are ineffective, and the effort futile.

I remember once asking my three-year-old daughter to get my tennis racket from the back entry and was startled when she asked, "Daddy, what's a tennis racket?" I explained, with gestures, that it was a piece of wood with a big loop at one end which had a lot of strings that went criss-cross in the loop. She responded with great enthusiasm and rushed out to the kitchen and came running back with my fish net. She was disappointed when I explained that the strings had to be tight so I could hit a ball with them, but she bounced right back into action and returned with my squash racket. Frustration, ineffectiveness, and futility were very much in evidence. The tennis racket finally turned up in the attic where I had personally stored it for safekeeping.

Such unfortunate experiences are very much to be avoided if we are to keep enthusiasm at the continuous high level necessary to accelerate our profitable growth.

Our Own Action Program

The program of action in our company has to be right for us. When deliberate planning and scheduling of improvement activities start at the top, they reflect the sincere desire of the executive leadership to unify the overall improvement effort and to eliminate the little kingdoms and ivory towers of fragmentation by independent specialties. Top management thus communicates that it is accepting its responsibility to coordinate innovation.

Long-range plans are delineated and communicated in such a

way that everyone can match his own goals with those of the company. Educational programs are designed to bring out the highest level of competence throughout the organization and avoid obsolescence by keeping everyone aware of the latest techniques applicable in each area of responsibility. When the educational part of the process is continuous and under the leadership of the manager in charge, training takes the form of "learning by doing" with today's real problems and opportunities the vehicle for development. The training specialists become staff assistants to the manager and play a supporting role as a resource with a much greater impact as the relevance of the "live cases" takes on greater meaning for everyone.

Executive Reflectivity

Top management action reflects downward. When a top executive shifts his support from one improvement activity this year to another the next and then fails to identify his own improvement efforts as part of either of them, he conveys a policy of ambivalence which can only be interpreted as his not knowing what he really wants of himself or his colleagues. Each manager who works for him shifts his emphasis in order to try to please the boss, and uncertainty reflects all the way down the line. Improvement activities [fluctuate wildly]—up one day, down the next. . . .

The truly professional manager, on the other hand, shows little tendency to shift his emphasis in such an erratic manner. He has few emergencies and crash programs because he knows where he is going and takes pride in his own participation with his people in reaching these goals.

Under such leadership long-range plans for improvement are codified into projections of profitable growth. Opportunity areas are identified in regular "developmental meetings" at all levels and are then passed up or down to the appropriate action point where the most effective treatment can be implemented. Staff specialists, and occasionally outside consultants, are brought in to help as needed.

The leadership in each division, department, and subgroup within the department assumes the responsibility for improvement in its own areas. Projects of greatest importance are given priority for review and approval up the line. Commitments to progress are established with schedules for reviews and completion dates. The latter becomes a vital part of the scorekeeping.

The reporting of results is no longer a numbers game when its purpose is understood as a tool for better planning and more accurate projecting of the improvement rate the next time around. The real measure of overall performance is understood to be the last line on the P & L statement, whereas the departmental effectiveness is measured as a variance from budget.

Participation in special task forces and interdepartmental teams can readily be reported back in regular departmental review meetings and thus become a method of communication. Everyone likes to know what is going on and shares in an added measure of satisfaction and recognition as he contributes on a broader base.

Promotions and Advancement

Through it all the recognition of the individual is greatest for his contribution to the total effort. Whether we like it or not, it is a competitive world and those who can perform best will move up. In the better-managed companies that way up is rarely a straight line. Movement from staff to line and back again as well as into different departments or disciplines has a fantastically broadening effect. Men on the move within any company meet more and different types of people and become involved in a greater variety of opportunities. Our strengths stand out under these conditions and our weaknesses tend to diminish as our own personal programs for improvement develop us to fill these voids.

A Pervasive Trend

In my opinion, the professional manager and the mature industrial engineer will eventually be one and the same person. Industrial engineering principles thus will become the thread that ties together the action phases of improvement management. People and techniques will be combined according to plan as a way of managing for profitable growth and total effectiveness.

The industrial engineer will become a professional manager by broadening his horizons, not narrowing them. His staff specialists will be the younger industrial engineers with a particular interest, but who work with the team, not off by themselves. His more experienced engineers will be men on the move which he fosters for the personal development and growth of the individual.

This approach is spreading throughout the modern company, including such areas as research and marketing. Supervisors, trained in industrial engineering by their own executive leadership, are already running departments in the plants of our unknown competitors. Direct employees are beginning to accept greater responsibility as they identify themselves more clearly as members of the company team. It is moving fast, and we cannot afford to bet on the wrong horse in the new game.

There will always be high-level specialists and certain sophisticated and glamorous techniques, but many of these techniques will shortly lose their glamor as their application becomes routinized. Others will most certainly take their place and new specialties will emerge. The professional manager, as an industrial engineer, will always have that delicate task of keeping the specialists in harmony with the coordinated effort of the whole organization.

CONCLUSIONS

We will continue to get the greatest thinking from the people who have the most brains, but we will also continue to get the greatest power of movement toward our objective of profitable growth when all of the people work more effectively together as a team.

The future of industrial engineering is pregnant with opportunities for men of vision who see the changing trends and have the wisdom and humility to move with them. The swing toward managing improvement according to plan becomes clearer every day. Changes in all areas will have to be more what people need and want rather than precisely what some of us think should be good for them. As mutual understanding, confidence, and respect grow everywhere they will most certainly converge.

One of Professor Erwin H. Schell's profound analogies sums it all up beautifully:

> We must ride the waves of change. . . . A skilled practitioner takes his surfboard out from the shallows as far as two miles from shore. When an incoming wave reaches a certain point, he mounts the board ahead of the wave and rides his way into the beach, a two-mile jaunt. He doesn't change the wave; he doesn't alter it; he doesn't fight it. He capitalizes on it.[5]

Remember—the surfboard rider is ahead of the wave, not behind it.

---

[5] Ibid., p. 65.

Too Much Management, Too Little Change

Leo B. Moore

Leo B. Moore is professor of management, Sloan School of Management, MIT. His concern for professional performance at every organizational level culminated in his efforts at setting up the Improvement Institute. Mr. Moore has been actively involved with it and with other engineering and management societies.

Managers are always looking for ways to do things better. Their prayer is, "If we can *only* keep six months ahead of the competition. . . ." As individuals they tend to have a deep-rooted sense of possibilities for improvement and to possess the knack of coupling new ideas with old situations to gain an important advantage. But knowing that they cannot leave improvement to chance, to opportunity, or to inspiration, they plan for it carefully. They establish various kinds of activities expressly designed for effecting improvement in and around the main stream of finance, production, and marketing.

Whether they are called industrial or product engineering, cost reduction or waste elimination, quality or budgetary control, these activities generally enjoy only a staff status. The people assigned to them operate on the strength of their convictions and on the truth of the facts as they see them; such is the basis of their advice to the line. In their specific areas they set out to in-

Leo B. Moore, "Too Much Management, Too Little Change," *Harvard Business Review,* January–February 1956. Copyright © 1956 by the President and Fellows of Harvard College; all rights reserved.

vestigate, evaluate, analyze, decide, and recommend—a procedure that is as sound as it is traditional.

However, no matter how many "bright boys," experts, and specialists are in the improvement groups, somehow, when the manager checks up, not much seems to be going on. Instead of looking hard at the line to find opportunities for improvement, the staff men spend most of their time performing repetitive work or running errands for the line. Industrial engineers are setting rates in endless numbers, at the same time trying to cope with one rush job after another imposed by management. Cost reduction figurers are battling to save pennies, and letting dollars go down the drain. Development men are busy trying to make a research idea work, while a competitor scoops the market by meeting the obvious demands of customers.

Management will not long remain content with these conditions, and soon will seek ways of correcting them. It begins to plead for increased emphasis on improvement, for more constructive work. To support its efforts it calls upon the three C's—conversation, contests, consultants—all aimed at providing a lift and a purpose to the improvement effort. The impact of these methods on the business is most gratifying for the length of time that they are employed; but as soon as they are dropped, the enthusiasm and the gains drop with them. Lethargy grows. The old routine reasserts itself. And the managers become frustrated and disgusted. What is the explanation? Where have things gone wrong? Whose fault is it?

FUTILITY OF PRESSURE

The reason why improvement efforts fizzle out, according to one school of thought, is that workers are not interested in change. This view is amazingly popular. To support it, evidence is produced that people (below managers) have no ideas and suggest nothing worthwhile day in and day out. Yet I know a foreman accused of lacking interest in new methods who holds several patents in a field different from that of his own company. An-

85

other unenthusiastic foreman does the finest cabinet work I have ever seen, in a shop at his home. Another is a painter of such talent as to exhibit and sell his output. And in each case management had no knowledge of the man's creative interests.

Another and more logical-sounding explanation is that people's natural reaction to the new is an automatic and definite negative reaction—not just lack of interest, but actual resistance to change. This too seems to be supported by evidence. People laughed at Fulton and his steamboat; Vanderbilt scorned Westinghouse and his air brake; the automobile was shouted down with the cry, "Go get a horse!" In our own times people have derided the safety of the airplane, sneered at streamlining automobiles, joked about Buck Rogers's rocket travel.

I question, however, whether this is resistance to *change* as much as it is resentment or anxiety over *the way change is introduced.* Trying to convince someone of the advantages of the new method often results in sounding like criticism of the old— which the person likes because he is accustomed to it, or which he may even be proud of because he sponsored it originally. More than one foreman has flatly rejected a new machine by saying, either in anger or in hurt, that there is nothing wrong with the performance of his department. Also, sometimes the change is introduced in such a way that it appears to threaten established work habits and relationships; it never gets a chance to be accepted in its own right. Many a supervisor has made a new process turn out to be just as impractical as he predicted it would be.

PUTTING THE HEAT ON

Faced with what looks like lack of interest or resistance, managers usually decide that the impulse for improvement must come from the top; that the forces involved are the same as in any other work program and must be handled through the regular management functions of planning, organizing, directing, coordinating, and controlling; that the responsibility for getting action cannot be shared since the need for improvement is not motive enough; and that the only way to get progress is to keep after it.

Accordingly, management presses the improvement groups, argues and fights with them until the logjam of inertia and inactivity is broken, and then keeps the heat on. In a typical manager's meeting with his various groups, discussion revolves around what needs to be done and how it can be done sooner, with an incessant squeezing and rapier-like questioning until commitments are made and some assurance is gained that action is in the offing. Between meetings, the push is maintained by tickler file and office memo so that promises made will be kept.

The mood that is created is one of action and energy. I have seen industrial engineers committing themselves, against their better judgment, to putting rates on all operations of a process within two days when five would have been a better estimate; sales analysts setting higher quotas for the salesmen without taking the time to consult the district sales managers; even research and development groups, usually considered free from such pressures, agreeing to produce answers by a specified date.

Yet, for all the effort and energy that is expended, the results are never truly satisfying to the manager. Ulcers are developed to justify small advances. What should be fun is turned into a chore. Although the managers spend more time pressing for improvement than they do in carrying out their other functions, the utter futility and wastefulness of the effort escapes them in their anxiety to make progress.

NEW PHILOSOPHY

What can managers do about this situation? Certainly it is up to them to do something, for it does not look as if the trends of the times will make matters any easier for them. As we look ahead into the not too distant future, it is becoming clearly evident that, with a greater population demanding greater production from a

87

smaller proportion of productive workers, the pressure will be on for increased output per man-hour. It is equally clear that this step-up in productivity must come from new methods and manufacturing techniques.

From the manager's point of view the picture is even more alarming because his company must move faster just to keep up with changes from outside. On the one side, consumers want new models oftener, and a greater variety in each model; on the other side, competition forces more mechanization, which makes it harder to adjust to the market. The mounting rate at which all sorts of changes, both technological and sociological, are developing imposes a need for accelerated improvement in every company, large or small.

Even more important is the fact that all these changes affecting business are no longer minor but fundamental, and so far-reaching that managers cannot afford to wait for some company to develop the techniques and then pick up from there. The impact of automation is a dramatic example, but only one. More basic know-how must be built into the organization merely to copy or reproduce the efforts of others.

Clearly then managers must take improvement out of the domain of uncertainty and exercise their administrative and organizational wit to meet the future on its own terms.

NEED FOR NEW ATTITUDE

Perhaps the first and most important area for the manager to investigate is his own attitude toward improvement and its accomplishment. We know that managers like and want improvement; yet managers do some strange things in this area.

For example, one inconsistent attitude is the all-embracing belief in action. This is the presumption that production must produce, marketing must market, and finance must finance; by inference—and often by words and deeds—any diversion of interest is frowned on. I heard one plant manager scold the supervisor of the machine shop for experimenting with a gadget for the production department; when all the work orders were completed, *then* the supervisor could try out some of his fancy ideas, the manager said.

Yet if you ask managers whether the line has improvement responsibility, they will with one voice assure you that this is true, adding that all improvement groups merely serve as staff to the line. "The line is and must be improving all the time," said one vice-president, "because the line is close to the problems." This attitude sounds fine, unless you ask whether any line man has ever been fired for not improving and whether any means now exists for measuring and evaluating the improvement activity of the line organization.

How can there be much improvement when management takes the attitude that a man must keep busy or be judged a slacker? I am thinking of the plant where foremen get on the move when the plant superintendent appears over the horizon simply because this is the thing to do. Every manager knows that creativity needs a favorable climate, and in the case of research many of them have spent endless dollars for facilities just to provide that climate. Yet I know of one company where the desks of the foremen were taken away because it was felt they should be on their feet and out in the midst of their troubles; and in another company the engineers lost their movable-partition offices for the same reason. Did any man ever find an answer of any consequence while he was in the midst of his troubles?

All of these people have time for improvement, *but they need the feeling that time spent on improvement is time well spent.* The "let's stop thinking and start doing" attitude on the part of managers has done more to stifle initiative and creativity in industry than any single other factor.

BASIC DESIRE OF PEOPLE

The belief that people do not have ideas and are not interested in improvement is as absurd as the opinion voiced so many times by people below managers that "they don't want new ideas around here." Three truths should be common knowledge for managers; they should become a natural and basic operating philosophy in every approach to improvement.

1. Workers and supervisors generally possess the same feelings about improvement as managers do. Everyone likes to improve. The urge to do better lies deep inside us all; it is an outstanding American characteristic. We play golf and keep a score at the same time. People view human activity in terms of progress—development and advancement.

2. Everyone likes to join. Human beings run together because every human urge is satisfied in terms of other people. They find their greatest gratification in association with other folk under any name or aim, improvement included, that provides opportunity to be, think, and act with others.

3. Everyone likes to contribute or experience a sense of contribution. Consultants are frequently accused of getting ideas from everyone in the company and putting these ideas for improvement in a shape suitable for presentation to management. Consultants know that people like to put forth their ideas, and they take advantage of it by simply asking people for their thoughts. The fact that they do provide a channel of communication to management is simply happenstance. The significant thing is that the ideas are there for them to find in the first place.

Many managers have instituted programs that have tended to take advantage of these truths—for example, the extensive training efforts of our businesses, certain types of rating and evaluation programs, and suggestion systems. However, while such programs appeal to the desires of people to improve, join, and contribute—and therefore often stir up a warm response, at least in the early stages—they are seldom really based on these desires. Foreman-training courses are designed without consulting the foremen to find out what they think they need to be trained in; evaluation programs afford little opportunity for workers and supervisors to join in outlining the rating procedures; suggestion systems tend to be impersonal and arbitrary.

It is no wonder then that the employee cooperation programs

fall just as flat as the efforts of the improvement groups. Although the managers may react to this with publicity, preaching, and sometimes pained expressions, which at frequent intervals inject new life and vigor into the programs, the new-found vitality always wears off and the programs once again await new pushes.

MANAGERS' BLIND SPOTS

At this point managers can hardly be blamed for becoming more convinced than ever that improvement comes from pressure. What else seems to work? But here they miss the real point. People do not resist change and they do not resent criticism. They resist *being* changed and they resent *being* criticized; they resist being pushed into change and they resent being hammered with criticism. But they do *not* resist change as such. In fact, they accept it. They await the new models of automobiles, refrigerators, and ranges, and are critical if the new models are not very different from last year's. They change their political leanings and even their religion. They seek education and skill, experiences and ideas, gadgets and devices. The new physical and chemical developments have fired their imaginations beyond belief. (My youngest son looking at the new moon one evening with me said, "Daddy, I want to go there," and my answer to him was a simple statement that he probably could some day.)

We have all heard people criticize themselves. Some people I know criticize themselves vehemently. They hold their smallest failures up for all to see and make a fetish of their apparent stupidity. They tell stories about themselves with great glee and seem to embellish their foolishness without shame.

What managers have overlooked, then, is that people do really like change and do not mind criticism *if they make these changes and these criticisms themselves.* This applies to everyone, not just those below the manager. I have seen vice-presidents resist and resent the proposals of their presidents in

91

the same way that everyone else does, and then throw themselves into programs of their own.

We can now see the reason for the leveling out of the results accomplished by the improvement groups in a company. These groups are made up of experts. They know and have all the answers. And they do not mind telling you that they know their business (which is true). But having an answer and putting it into effect are different and separate pieces of business. Every one of the groups represents push to those with whom it comes in contact. Countless stories can be told of the resistance, insidious as it is and disadvantageous as it may be, put up by the line to staff groups in their attempts to introduce improvements. The experts are scorned just as the manager is scorned when he uses "I'll tell them" techniques.

TECHNIQUES OF GROUP ACTION

What does all this mean for the manager? It means, I am convinced, that if he wants a real will to improvement in his division, he must turn to the techniques of joint action and participation. Now, "participation" is an overworked word. It has been distorted so often in pious speeches and house organ editorials, and it has been applied so often as a gimmick or a manipulative device, that to some it even has bad connotations. Still, it comes closer to describing the concept I have in mind than any other word in the dictionary, so for lack of a better term I shall use it here.

Participation provides the opportunity for self-criticism and, through it, for initiating and instituting changes in the methods, procedures, and techniques of the members of the group. It permits a sense of contribution and joining with others for a common purpose. It furnishes a motive for real concern about the areas best known to the group members—their own work. The results of the group effort provide a large recognition for the members who collaborated. The teamwork releases much of the latent abilities of the participants in a dedicated, rewarding search for improvement.

For example, a group of women went to a meeting led by their foreman and attended by the product engineer. The problem was how to increase the output of their assembly operation. "If the mounting holes were moved a half inch in this direction, we could use a holding fixture," the women pointed out. "And if this part were changed to give clearance, we could assemble from bottom up and do two at a time." Doubtless the engineers could have figured out this improvement themselves if they had studied the situation. The trouble is, of course, that like anyone else they cannot think of everything and do not have time for everything. In this case, it is not hard to imagine that the women got a real kick out of making engineering changes too.

The manager who decides to use participation as a means toward improvement must enter into the process in the mood of seeking aid and counsel. At the same time, he is not just a mediator or arbitrator, but a leader of a team operating in a permissive atmosphere that he creates. The team members are expected by him to make contributions and to express their thoughts freely and without prejudice. The manager encourages the members of the group to state their views on all facets of the issues under consideration in order to arrive at harmonious decisions on these issues of mutual concern. Their views are sought because the manager believes that their ideas are important and are needed; and he must feel this, not just pretend it.

For years I have watched one administrator exercise consummate skill in communicating his sincere desire for the thoughts and ideas of his group. You can see it best in the treatment of the newcomer. At the first meeting of the group the executive selects some topic with which the new man is familiar and at ease. Throughout every discussion he always goes around the room making certain that everyone voices his opinion, but he keeps the new man in mind particularly. For instance, he usually starts with him by making some remark which indicates the newcomer's status and fresh viewpoint. In this way, the oldsters do not and cannot shut up the youngster, and the youngster knows that he belongs and is expected to contribute.

Participation does not mean winning friends and influencing people. Rather, it is analogous to the good salesman's sincere concern for the potential customer. Even more basically, it is a means for the company to exercise its responsibility to the people who work there—to provide its people with a sense of belonging based on human dignity.

GETTING STARTED

Many managers hesitate to introduce participation on an organized and regular basis because it is not easy to initiate. Obviously, it will not do to call a meeting and say, "Let's participate," if for years the manager has been a dominant "tell 'em" man. The group would not know how to accept it and would react with suspicion, if not fear. When there is a background of relations that have not been friendly or free, a fundamental change in relationships must be made before anything constructive can take place.

Usually this means a change in the manager himself and in his techniques. Needless to say, this is hard both on the executive and on his associates who suffer through the transition with him, but experience at least indicates that the "payoff" will not be long in coming. Once the group under the executive senses the change, it will be most anxious to go along in the effort.

Other managers balk at the idea of group action because it seems strange. A little reflection will show that the concept is far from novel. It is the glue that holds together gangs, clubs, and unions. Youngsters, from the time they join the Little League ball club, gang together to steal apples, or form a little theater group, are well familiar with group action. When mothers band together to clean up some unhealthful condition in the streets or to supervise playground activity for the children, they use the group idea to get results. There are countless other examples—the old-fashioned barn-raising in a New England farm community, the

94

tremendous group spirit and endeavor during World War II, the community action when tragedy, hurricane, or sickness strikes.

But in their working hours in plants and offices, people see so little of group effort. Why? The fact that participation is not used in our businesses rests with the managers on every level. I have long felt that they are deterred largely because of their preconceptions. The thought of the manager asking for advice goes against the administrative grain. As the boss, he thinks that he cannot show those under him that he does not know all the answers. He cannot ever let them take control away from him for he will lose his managerial position, or at least his status.

Some managers with such preconceptions defend their position by saying that they *do* have participation. "In every one of my meetings I ask people what they think," they will tell you. But if you should attend those meetings, it becomes very clear that the only ones who dare answer are the "yes men." The others have learned that they get burned if they voice any objection or suggest that some other answer may be available.

The manager who wishes to get participation started should logically begin with a situation that is not too complex, political, or emotional. If possible, it should be obvious, both to him and the group members, that he could benefit from the advice of those around him. A slow, easy start is better than a sensational beginning, for this is a great change.

He may come out in the open and state the change and ask the group to help, on the basis that confession is good for the soul and prompts sympathetic cooperation; or he may want to get his feet a bit wet before committing himself to the change since, being human, he like everyone else resists being pushed into the new. In the latter case he might start asking people for ideas and then listen them out. This technique is perfect for breaking up yes-man conferences and developing constructive ideas.

For example, a plant superintendent who had become conscious of his tendency to run the meeting decided to change his tactics: he would ask for ideas and suggestions and then shut up. After a painful silence during which the yes men were moving

95

their heads the other way, looking for someone to speak up, two supposed incompetents quietly but definitely took a long-standing situation apart, called a spade a spade, and laid out a possible solution as neatly as a trained surgeon performs an appendectomy. The superintendent listened, goggle-eyed and amazed.

CONFERENCE METHOD

Nothing interferes more with participation and group action than having a meeting with no clear purpose in front of the group. It is the duty of the manager as the leader to state the topic of the conference in clear, simple words. This statement should include the areas that are in-bounds and out-of-bounds. Advance notice, preferably in a written memorandum, should be given to the group members. These members should be selected on the basis of their interest in the topic before the group and their ability to contribute to it. Beware of leaving out an individual who should be in attendance.

Also, the facilities should be conducive to creative thinking and positive decision making. The room, the lights, the ventilation, and the writing equipment—all should be suitable to the occasion. Very important to a successful conference is protection against interruptions. Why do so many conference rooms have telephones that deliver incoming calls?

The leader should employ an organized conference-leading technique, and this technique should be known and understood by the participants. Any of the well-known conference arts that involve a pattern approach will suffice. They are not difficult to learn, and skill in their use is acquired through practice. These conference techniques have a step-by-step pattern which will take the meeting through a review of the situation, a determination of the problem or problems involved, a listing of possible solutions to each problem, a selection of the most promising solutions, and an agreement on the course of action to implement the solutions.

However, the manager should not hesitate to enter into the

participative process for lack of conference leadership training. Let the group help here. The main advantage of the conference technique lies in the clarity of approach and the speed of action which together reduce the length of meetings and the number that are nonproductive. And obviously there is a lot more to it, whether on an instinctive or on a planned basis, than I can indicate here.

TIMING OF GROUP ACTION

When in the decision process should an executive call for group thinking and action?

The simple and general answer is: *at that time when a problem situation becomes known to the manager and his group.* For instance, the marketing people relay some data on a product indicating a probable increase in demand; an incoming letter makes it clear that quality has slipped; or safety, production, and cost reports may point to trends that require action. A meeting of the people who are involved in and concerned with the situation should be called as soon as possible.

The group members may want time to prepare themselves for the meeting, but delay should be held to a minimum so that the situation will not become critical and put pressure on the manager to avoid group action. Whether a manager anticipates a problem situation or senses some appropriate course of action in the future, it is desirable to receive the benefit of group thinking and to permit group planning. Conferences of this nature build a cohesiveness in the manager's group that defies emergencies and tends to eliminate fire-fighting assignments.

How often should a group meet? Again the answer is simple: *as often as needed to gain acceptance and approval of the proposed course of action.* This does not mean that meetings are held until everyone goes down to defeat or capitulates. It only means that meetings continue until substantial disagreement has been resolved, until the sense and temper of the group thinking has jelled into general understanding and common accord. It is wise for the leader of a group to break a large problem situation into manageable parts so that the very complexity of the situation and the interdependence of the problems involved do not leave the group with a sense of frustration and indecision.

SUITABLE PROBLEMS

The manager himself decides what problems are submitted to a group for participation and action. Logically, suitable problem areas would be those in which the group may help the manager or those in which the group may reach a uniformity of opinion. No general rule can be made in this matter except to say that scarcely any restriction seems to exist. An amazing number and variety of situations have been the subject of participation and group action on all levels of management.

The willingness of the group to tackle any problem and the approaches that it takes in specific cases never cease to provide surprise and pleasure for the manager. In turn, the group may at times be more direct or more demanding than a manager would ever dare to be. Here are just a few instances of what participation has achieved.

Groups made up of foremen, assistant foremen, supervisors, gang bosses, and the like have, through participation, developed and installed improvements in manufacturing methods, scheduling, materials handling, record keeping, and better tools, jigs, fixtures, workplace layouts—the whole gamut of the production activity. In one case a group reviewing an assembly problem discovered that an assembly made for a branch plant was promptly disassembled before being used there. The group recommended eliminating the assembly operation and putting the operators on other work.

Another company planning an expansion invited help from the foreman group in deciding where to locate the new plant and which foremen to transfer to it. The foremen joined in a study of alternatives, recommended a new location, and drew up a list of their number to be assigned there. At that point the layout of the plant came up for discussion. The participation of the employees of the department which was to be expanded into the new plant was requested. The group pored over drawings, made three-dimensional models, and recommended changes in facilities, equipment, layout, parking areas, services, and other matters that reduced the bill for the new plant considerably.

A company wanted to introduce a rating and evaluation program for middle-management people as a part of its executive development program. Rating systems from consultants were available, but the problem was turned over to the group to be rated and the members developed their own system, which was more stringent than any proposed by outside firms.

Still another company, in the sales field, put the problem of territory boundaries, quotas, and commissions before a representation of its sales force. This group made recommendations to management which showed real insight into the problem and also an understanding of its intricate detail. The group also suggested that it administer and review the matter at regular intervals.

In the office, groups have reviewed records, reports, forms, methods, procedures, and equipment; hundreds of examples of improvement in paperwork through participation are known. For example, one office group found a lengthy report that had been compiled by it for some time and distributed monthly in a large quantity but which was no longer used or needed in the company. It was quickly eliminated and the personnel released to more meaningful activity.

Group action also provides an opportunity for different staff and line groups to work together. For example, in one company a group composed of members of the production, design, and development engineering functions, together with representatives from manufacturing, have reviewed product lines with an eye to cost reduction, standardization, and other forms of improvement.

In a case of technological impact on a firm, a group in a large railroad studied the re-layout and re-equipping of repair facilities for locomotives necessitated by the changeover from steam to diesel power. The final recommendation to management was reviewed by the board of directors, which promptly endorsed the whole plan.

I have purposely chosen examples of joint action at the employee and middle-management level, because there participation is a good deal less common than in upper-management circles. Board meetings and executive group meetings tend to be participative (although they are not necessarily so), as do junior boards and advisory committees. It is amazing and mystifying that the senior managers have not permitted their philosophy to filter down to the lower levels.

SELF-IMPOSED LIMITS

All restrictions on the use of participation center on the manager himself. The manager should not use the technique if the answer to the problem is known to him. The idea that we use participation of the group to convince its members of the rightness of the decision already reached is repugnant to the basic principles of seeking aid and advice. Other forms of manipulation—i.e., discipline, censure, pressure, influence—all fall in the same category.

The group should not be used by the manager to shirk his own responsibility. If the final decision rests with him, then he must shoulder the responsibility for that decision and not hide behind the group in the event that the recommendation turns out to be a poor one. The manager does not embarrass the group by encouraging members to recommend action in areas beyond their power. He does not push them out over their heads in order to gain time or provide a shield for his own future.

By far the most restrictive force on the manager is belief and faith. A manager who does not believe in the worthwhileness of participation and the capabilities of his group to think and act with courage, foresight, and conviction might just as well not begin. In like manner, no manager should expect results by ordering participation, by directing it, or by controlling it. A manager must really believe completely; otherwise he loses the most important part—the group members' enthusiasm for continuing to contribute, and their willingness to keep on trying to improve.

CONCLUSION

The long-run advantage of participation and group action does not lie primarily in the eye-opening results that it achieves, nor in the glittering newness that it imparts, but in the clear evidence that it offers of democracy in business. This is not lip-service democracy but a practical demonstration of cooperative effort. It is effective because it appeals to human desires and needs, hangs on a fundamental belief or faith in people, and releases their latent abilities for a worthwhile purpose. Last but not least, it establishes a sound basis for renewed faith in our business and industry as a way of life.

Selected Readings

Appley, Lawrence A. *Management in Action—The Art of Getting Things Done Through People.* New York: American Management Association, 1956.

Argyris, Chris. *Integrating the Individual and the Organization.* New York: John Wiley, 1964.

Argyris, Chris. *Personality and Organization.* New York: Harper & Row, 1957.

Barnes, Ralph M. *Motion and Time Study.* 6th ed. New York: John Wiley, 1968.

Clark, Wallace. *The Gantt Chart: A Working Tool of Management.* 3rd ed. London: Sir Isaac Pitman & Sons Ltd., 1952.

Drucker, Peter F. *The Practice of Management.* New York: Harper & Row, 1954.

Gardner, B. B., and Moore, D. G. *Human Relations in Industry.* 4th ed. Homewood, Ill.: Richard D. Irwin, 1964.

Gellerman, Saul W. *Motivation and Productivity.* New York: American Management Association, 1963.

Gilbreth, Lillian M. *The Quest for the One Best Way.* Easton, Pa.: Hive Publishing Co., reprint of 1928 edition.

Goodwin, Herbert F., and Moore, Leo B. *Management Thought and Action in the Words of Erwin H. Schell.* Cambridge, Mass.: MIT Press, 1967.

Graham, Ben S., Sr. *Work Simplification.* Tipp City, Ohio: Ben S. Graham Corp., reprint of 1956 edition.

Haire, Mason. *Psychology in Management.* New York: McGraw-Hill, 1956.

Lasieur, Fred G., ed. *The Scanlon Plan.* New York: John Wiley, 1958.

Likert, Rensis. *New Patterns of Management.* New York: McGraw-Hill, 1961.

Lincoln, James F. *Incentive Management.* Cleveland, Ohio: Lincoln Electric Co., 1951.

Maier, Norman R. F., and Hayes, John J. *Creative Management.* New York: John Wiley, 1962.

Maslow, Abraham H. *Motivation and Personality.* New York: Harper & Row, 1954.

McGregor, Douglas. *The Human Side of Enterprise.* New York: McGraw-Hill, 1960.

McGregor, Douglas. *The Professional Manager.* New York: McGraw-Hill, 1967.

Mogensen, Allan H. *Common Sense Applied to Motion and Time Study.* New York: McGraw-Hill, 1932.

Roethlisberger, F. J., and Dickson, W. J. *Management and the Worker.* Cambridge, Mass.: Harvard University Press, 1939.

Williams, Whiting. *Mainsprings of Man.* New York: Charles Scribner's Sons, 1925.

Williams, Whiting. *What's on the Worker's Mind.* New York: Arno Press, reprint of 1920 edition.

PART TWO
Current Trends
and Directions

Every Employee a Manager

M. Scott Myers

M. Scott Myers, Ph.D., director of the Center for Applied Management in Coral Gables, Florida, is a prime contributor to the research, development, and implementation of advanced management systems and job enrichment.

ORIGIN OF THE TWO-CLASS SYSTEM

The management-labor adversary relationship is an extension of the two-class system which dates back to the dawn of history. Ancient history makes reference to master-slave and landlord-serf relationships. Royalty-commoner and officer-soldier are enduring manifestations of ancient two-class systems. In the middle ages the journeyman-apprentice relationship gradually evolved with capitalism to the management-labor dichotomy which characterizes labor relations in most organizations.

The two-class system is largely a function of discrepancies between the upper and lower classes in terms of knowledge and wealth. Generally speaking, members of the upper class had more knowledge and wealth than members of the lower class. Knowledge, as it is used in this context, refers to the body of knowledge embraced by the ruling class. Thus, the official religion of the ruling class may not always have passed the test of rational scrutiny, but it was the body of knowledge that justified

This paper is an update of a paper originally published in the *California Management Review* and is excerpted from the manuscript of a book entitled *Managing With Unions,* published by Addison-Wesley, 1978.

the annihilation of infidels, no matter how scientific the basis for their conflicting knowledge. Knowledge, to be acceptable, must fit the norms of the day. Socrates, for example, was ahead of his time and lost his life because his knowledge challenged the accepted wisdom of the ruling class. However, in most cases the knowledge of the upper classes had a better foundation in objectivity than the superstition and folklore-oriented knowledge of the lower classes.

The two-class system tended to be self-perpetuating, as moneyed members of society had the means and discretionary time to pursue knowledge and to qualify for leadership roles in government, the military, clergy, education, and commerce. The lower class, continuously preoccupied with subsistence, had little time or opportunity to gain membership in the upper class. Indeed, should happenstance suddenly endow a member of the early American lower class with money, he, as a *nouveau-riche,* would be vulnerable to rejection by the closed fraternity of the established upper class. This rejection occurred not only because of his humble background, but also because his knowledge orientation identified him philosophically, politically, socially, and economically with the lower class.

In early America, the blue-collar worker characteristically lived in a world circumscribed by oppression and ignorance. The label "working stiff" accurately reflected his commercial value as brawn rather than brain. Child labor, 18-hour days, and six-day weeks were his normal expectations. Pay rates of blue-collar workers were typically less than one-fourth the pay levels of white-collar workers. Many blue-collar workers were illiterates or immigrants with language handicaps. Of course, communications media as we know them today—newspapers, magazines, moving pictures, radio, and television—were not part of the life experience of early Americans. Indeed, reading experience in the literate household was often limited to the Bible and other moralistic publications. Hence, members of the working class had little time or energy to pursue life enrichment, nor would they, with their circumscribed perspective, know what to pursue if given the opportunity. Many oppressed workers accepted their lot in life as though it were the natural order of things as prescribed by the deity—going to their ultimate deaths never realizing they were the victims of a giant rip-off.

EMERGENCE OF THE ADVERSARY RELATIONSHIP

The two-class system was in full force in early America before the influence of labor legislation and collective bargaining began ameliorating the situation of exploited wage earners. When Samuel Gompers and, later, William Haywood launched their unionization efforts in the latter part of the nineteenth century, they based their strategies on the assumption that management and labor have differing and contradictory goals. Gompers, Haywood, and other early union leaders didn't create the two-class system—they merely described the reality existing in early America, and had the insight and temerity to lead a revolt against economic tyranny.

Labor legislation and collective bargaining gradually began ameliorating the plight of the working man. A third force—mass production technology—simultaneously began pricing more goods within reach of wage earners, thereby upgrading the quality of life of the working man's family. Unfortunately, mass production work systems sometimes had adverse psychological impact on worker job satisfaction and productivity. Frustrated workers, now protected by labor laws and unions, began expressing their talents in counterproductive pursuits, thereby undermining much of the anticipated gains of mass production technology.

THE WORKER'S CHANGING PERSPECTIVE

As the working man's pay escalated and his leisure time increased, he moved in his needs hierarchy from subsistence or maintenance needs to higher-order needs for growth, achievement, responsibility, and recognition. By 1950, his horizons were broadened and his self-awareness deepened by a multiplicity of media. Many workers had just returned from widely dispersed involvement in World War II; they had access to radio, television, newspapers, periodicals, and movies in a society of increasing liberalism and permissiveness.

Television undoubtedly was the greatest single impact on the perceptions of the working man. During the 1950s, television became available to almost any American who wanted it. TV antennae appeared on the roofs of the lowliest ghetto shanty, as well as on the homes of the well-to-do. In the beginning, members of the lower socioeconomic strata tended to watch cartoons, comedies, and westerns, while the more formally educated tended more toward newscasts, educational programs, and fine arts. However, many lower-class members soon tired of slapstick fare and began watching a wider variety of programs. If they found educational programs interesting, it was due in part to the fact that no one told them they were "educational." Hence, program preferences of viewers in all classes gradually began coalescing toward a common fare.

ADVERSARIES SHARE A DATA BASE

For the first time in the known history of mankind, people of all classes had access to a common data base. Differences in class viewing preferences diminished as television began gradually raising the knowledge level of the culturally disadvantaged toward the level of the formally educated. Though personnel records continued to reflect great disparities in formal education, the perceptions and values of wage earners were becoming similar to those of the members of the managerial class. Indeed, some of the younger workers entering the workforce were more liberal, worldly, and sophisticated than the supervisors they reported to. But, these younger workers had spent more of their life in front of TV sets than had their supervisors, who were too busy in pursuit of Horatio Alger career goals to devote much time to TV. Thus, supervisors who acquired their leadership roles by conformity, obedience, loyalty, manipulation, and productivity were less well educated in some respects than the "ungrateful wretches" who entered the workforce seemingly with low commitment and high expectations.

The deterioration of the old work ethic was not simply a function of exposure to TV, of course, but was also a result of new perspectives arising from a combination of parental permissiveness, reaction to materialism, peer pressure, and selective perception. The interaction of these factors in an affluent and relief-oriented society did much to emasculate the Horatio Alger theory that one succeeded through hard work, honesty, ambition, perseverance, sacrifice, and loyalty. It was a case of incomplete or distorted information dispensed by TV, lean on economics and sociology, and heavy on commercials and programs developing and appealing to the hedonistic needs of man. Thus, the new generation came into organizations inadequately programmed to pursue a full life of responsible citizenship as it was prescribed by their predecessors.

THE OBSOLESCENCE OF MANAGEMENT PREROGATIVES

For all this distortion or incompatibility in life orientation, the new generation was in some respects better informed than many of the supervisors on whom they depended for self-actualization in the workplace. And while their supervisors might be better oriented toward the economics and politics of survival and success in the workplace, they often embraced a set of unflattering assumptions about man and how he should be motivated. However, the managers were in power and, exercising their official though self-defeating prerogatives, they tended to use persuasion, bribery, manipulation, and threats to get the "ungrateful wretches" to shape up and get in step. But, of course, this official "boss power" was matched by unofficial "people power" made official at times by the charters of labor unions.

Along with the closure of the knowledge gap noted above,

came a reduction in the income gap between management and labor. Largely through legislation and collective bargaining, blue-collar wages gradually rose to the level of the white-collar worker. Indeed, it is not uncommon to encounter first-line supervisors taking home smaller paychecks than the people they supervise.

Thus, at last, the blue-collar worker is essentially both as well informed and as well paid as the white-collar worker. Now, as never before, the psychological conditions are right for converting the adversary relationships between management and labor into collaboration. Were it not for the power of long-term cultural conditioning, the mutually exclusive definitions of management and labor could be easily fused.

THE PERSEVERING PARENT TAPES

Unfortunately, the win-lose, management-labor cleavage and its correlates left indelible imprints on the minds of the contestants. The parent tapes of managers are still programmed in terms of management prerogatives with parent-child strategies for maximizing performance by manipulating all company resources, particularly the people. The parent tapes of hourly paid workers and their union leaders are just as strongly programmed to react to authority and to exercise child-parent strategies to "get away with" doing as little as possible. Thus, we find well-informed members of management and labor potentially capable of synergizing their pursuits of common goals; but, instead, unwittingly victimizing themselves by perpetuating tradition in the pursuit of mutually exclusive goals.

WORK SYSTEMS

For many people, work is a necessary evil, a requirement for getting the money they need to buy the things they need. Organizations' goals are not their goals; their goals are variously related to

112

a better lifestyle *away* from the job. These personal goals are often expressed in tangible terms such as new homes, steady incomes, college educations, new automobiles, Caribbean cruises, and country club memberships.

For these people, any sense of achievement, growth, responsibility, and recognition is more often experienced away from the job. The failure of people to satisfy these higher-order needs on the job cannot be attributed to their inherent or natural characteristics but, rather, to the circumstances through which they relate to the organization.

Work systems are characteristically designed on the assumption that the people who operate them are not trustworthy. The systems designers admonish each other to "design the system on the assumption that the operators can't think." And, of course, it becomes a self-fulfilling prophecy when the operators fail to respond intelligently to their "idiot-proof" work systems. The systems designers point scornfully to the operators saying, "See how stupid they are; they never think!"

However, the operators do think—but, unfortunately, in retaliatory terms or about things away from the job, or how to get away from the job. Hence, they increase their trips to the water fountain, rest room, first aid center, and personnel department, and use up their sick leave. At work they think and talk about their bowling games, camping trips, school board memberships, church activities, do-it-yourself projects, avocational pursuits, and job-hopping plans. Or their thoughts find creative expression in counterproductive activities such as product sabotage, defiance of authority, concerted slowdowns, pilferage, complaints about working conditions, and preoccupation with real or imaginary grievances.

People at the upper levels of the organization meanwhile often derive meaning from their roles both on and off the job. Their work is intrinsically challenging and interesting, the most unpleasant and insidious part of their job being their futile attempts to motivate the "ungrateful wretches" at the lower levels of the organization.

On the assumption that people at all levels are potentially

113

Figure I. The management-labor dichotomy.

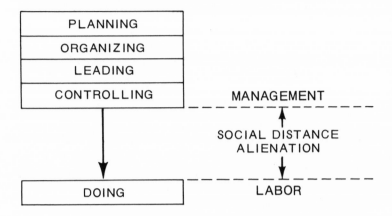

responsible and self-motivated, the mission is to create for the operators the same motivational opportunities experienced by managers. Make "every employee a manager" by enabling each person to manage a job commensurate with his latent capabilities and personal needs.*

People with meaningful roles in the organization meet their responsibilities in the same spirit that entrepreneurs pursue their organizational goals. In other words, the more a person's job resembles entrepreneurial responsibility, the more likely he or she will feel and act like a manager.

Consider, for example, the self-employed farmer who manages his own farm. In terms of the concept illustrated in Figure 1, his work does not create social distance or alienation, as he is representing the two sides of a responsibility which in some organizations is divided by a management-labor gap. However, if he employs helpers on his farm, they may or may not experience such a gap, depending on whether they are treated as "self-employed individuals" or as "hired hands."

But the farmer himself has a meaningful role, as illustrated in Figure 2. In the *plan* phase, he plans and organizes his seasonal

---

*M. Scott Myers, *Every Employee a Manager* (New York: McGraw-Hill, 1970).

cycle by developing a marketing strategy, determining acreage requirements, forecasting yields, readying equipment, prescribing pest controls, selecting seed, and crystallizing the planting schedule. He carries out his plans in the *do* phase by preparing the soil, planting the seeds, fertilizing, cultivating, applying pesticides, harvesting and marketing crops, and maintaining equipment. The *control* or feedback phase consists of measuring, evaluating, and correcting which, in this case, includes analysis of soil, yields, costs, profits, markets, and the inspection of equipment—all of which provide a basis for modifying next year's plan. He manages this total responsibility within constraints imposed by laws, technology, weather conditions, costs, human resources, schedules, and market conditions.

Figure 2. A model for meaningful work — farmer.

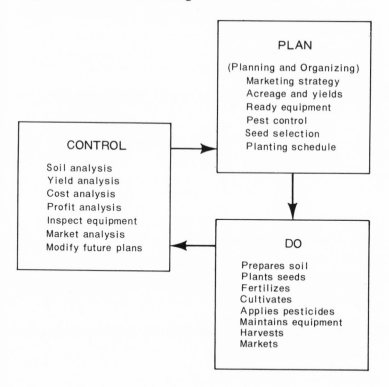

Figure 3. A model for meaningful work — operating vice president (division manager).

PLAN

R & D, manufacturing and
  marketing strategies
Inter-divisional interface
  strategies
Long-range organization and
  manpower planning
Facilities expansion
Implementation of manage-
  ment philosophy

CONTROL

Measures customer satis-
  faction
Reviews financial criteria
Evaluates facilities utiliza-
  tion
Audits morale and man-
  power development
Conducts project reviews
Analyzes economic and
  technological trend
Revises marketing strategies

DO

Meets key customers
Represents company to all
  publics
Coordinates and visits
  divisional operations
Communicates business in-
  formation
Maintains "open door"

Members of large organizations, particularly at the lower levels, rarely have the freedom or autonomy experienced by the self-employed entrepreneur. However, the closer to the top of the organization a person works, the more his job resembles that of a self-employed individual.

Figure 3 shows the plan-do-control phases of a division head who, as an operating vice president, is close to the top of the organization. He coordinates the planning of R & D, manufacturing and marketing strategies, interdivisional cooperative efforts, organizational development, and facilities expansion, and has a hand in shaping policy. The "doing" aspect of his job involves him with key customers, in public relations roles, visits to operating sites, the exchange of business information, and managing conflict. His control functions include the measurement, evaluation, and correction of factors associated with customer satisfaction, financial performance, facilities utilization, organization development, marketing strategies, and, of course, with legal constraints. Hence, the division director's job is rich in plan, do, and control, much like the self-employed individual.

Similarly, Figure 4 shows the middle-management job of a manufacturing manager—two levels below the division head—to be quite rich in terms of plan, do, and control. A company is rarely plagued with a poorly motivated manufacturing manager.

Even the foreman's job (first-level supervisor), two levels

Figure 4. A model for meaningful work — manufacturing manager.

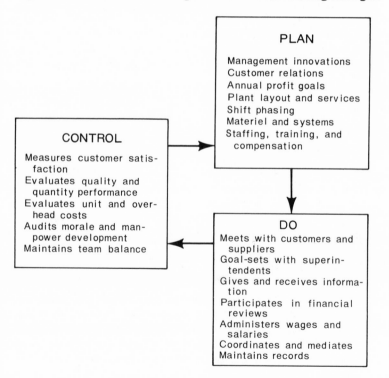

Figure 5. A model for meaningful work—foreman.

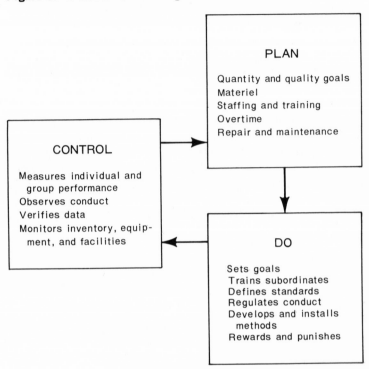

below the manufacturing manager, may be rich in terms of meaningful work concepts. For example, we see in Figure 5 that the foreman's job, though narrower in scope than the superintendent's, offers him considerable latitude in managing his work. Unfortunately, this job, though rich in plan-do-control for the foreman, usually offers little opportunity for the operator to have a meaningful role.

Under this foreman's leadership, and constraints imposed by company and union policy, the operator (Figure 6) lives in a world circumscribed by conformity pressures to follow instructions, work harder, obey rules, get along with people, and be loyal to the supervisor, the company, and the union—all of which tend to quash any satisfaction that work itself might otherwise offer. His role puts him in a category with materials and other nonhuman resources to be manipulated by others who use him to pursue their organizational goals. Conformity-oriented workers tend to behave like adolescents responding to the punishments and rewards of authoritarian parents, or as tribesmen responding to their tribal chieftain. Persons dissatisfied with organizationally imposed conformity may fight back through the power of the labor union. Union-imposed conformity, in turn, may result in rebellion in the ranks of the bargaining unit.

The foreman's job in some organizations is complicated by the role of the union steward who also has jurisdictional responsibility for the same people supervised by the foreman. The union leader, in turn, often faces the dilemma of being a subordinate of

Figure 6. Conformity-oriented workers.

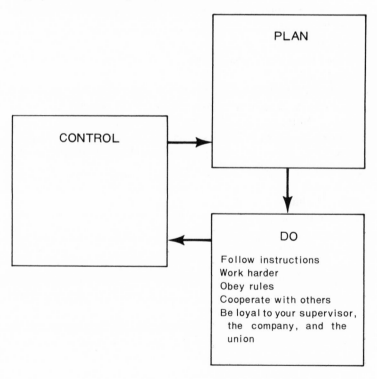

the foreman on matters of routine job performance but a peer, or even supervisor, on matters of union business. For instance, it is not uncommon for union leaders to have dealings with top management people with whom the foreman has little access. Thus it is understandable that employees (and their foreman also) often look first to the union steward as the best source of information. Thus, members of the bargaining unit may have, in effect, two supervisors who can put them in conflict situations, particularly if the shop steward and supervisor appear to be competing as adversaries for power in the organization. However, if union leaders and supervisors are committed in spirit and contract to a relationship of mutual respect and support, these role conflicts are not likely to occur.

Workers culturally conditioned to expect a boss, either company or union, to call the shots may find nothing unusual in the fact that their jobs have little or no planning and control functions. However, the knowledge explosion following World War II, coupled with the gradual displacement of older conformists by the younger enlightened, is making this type of subservient role unacceptable to increasing numbers in the workplace.

Thus, to adapt to the changing perceptions and expectations of the newer generations, the authority-dominated job shown in Figure 6 must be revised to include the planning and control functions illustrated in Figures 2–5.

Strategies for restructuring jobs to provide balanced plan-do-control responsibilities compatible with organizational requirements and jobholder capabilities and aspirations may be described in terms of three approaches: 1. jobholder approach; 2. task force approach; and 3. management approach.

Jobholder approach. When job incumbents are in methods improvement programs, such as the Mogensen Work Simplification process, it may be appropriate to include in this training program the concept of "every employee a manager" and the meaning of plan-do-control. With this orientation, they can begin analyzing their own jobs in terms of a sequence which begins with the sample items illustrated in Figure 7. After completing all items which have relevance to their kind of work, they can then

Figure 7. Worksheet for analyzing job content.

PLANNING. Can the individual or group —

Name customers and state delivery dates for products or services?
State the product quality and quantity commitments?
Organize their work layout and influence personnel assignments?
Set goals and standards based on customer needs, and fix priorities?
State the sources of their materials and problems in obtaining them?
List direct and overhead costs, selling price, and other profit
  and loss information?

DOING. Does the job —

Utilize their talents and require their attention?
Enable them to see the relationship of their work to other operations?
Provide access to all the information they need to do their work?
Have a satisfactory work cycle — neither too long nor too short?
Give people feedback on how well they are doing?
Enable them to see how they contribute to the usefulness of the
  product for the customer?

CONTROLLING. Can the individual or group —

State customer quality requirements and reasons for these standards?
Keep their own records of quality and quantity?
Check quality and quantity of work and revise procedures?
Evaluate and modify work layout on their own initiative?
Identify and correct unsafe working conditions?
Obtain information from people outside the group as a means of
  evaluating performance?

---

analyze items in terms of the three basic questions illustrated in Figure 8.

In addition, or as an alternative to this approach, job incumbents might be given an opportunity to enrich their job by taking appropriate items from their supervisor's job. After acquainting them with the plan-do-control concept, show them their supervisor's job as illustrated in Figure 5 and ask them, "Is there anything in your supervisor's job that you can do, and would like to do?" In a similar way they may be given the opportunity to ask for duties listed in the job descriptions of others such as inspectors and engineers. The enrichment of the operator's job through this process may lead to the partial impoverishment of the jobs from which their new responsibilities were selected.

The supervisor, in turn, may go through a similar experience

Figure 8. Job design checklist for incumbent.

PLANNING	No	Sometimes	Yes
Does my job allow me to set my own performance goals?	( )	( )	( )
Is setting my own goals essential to good job performance?	( )	( )	( )
Do I want more opportunity to set my own performance goals?	( )	( )	( )
DOING			
Does my job provide variety?	( )	( )	( )
Is variety in my job essential to good job performance?	( )	( )	( )
Do I want more variety in my work?	( )	( )	( )
CONTROLLING			
Does my job allow me to measure my work performance?	( )	( )	( )
Is opportunity to evaluate my own work essential?	( )	( )	( )
Do I want more opportunity to measure my own job performance?	( )	( )	( )

of evaluating his job and taking items from his supervisor's job to enrich his own. The net effect of such a process, as it moves continuously upward, is to make jobs more meaningful at every level. One effect of such a process is not only to enrich the operator's job, but also to change his relationship to his supervisor from a conformity-oriented to a goal-oriented relationship, as illustrated in Figure 9.

A comparison of the content of the operator's and supervisor's jobs in Figure 9 with the content of their jobs in Figures 5 and 6 shows each to be experiencing a more meaningful role and to be utilizing his talents more effectively. In other words, each has a job which resembles the model in Figure 2 and, to the extent that it does, each has a sense of working for himself.

The implementation of job enrichment cannot take place without influencing individuals in jobs adjacent to and directly above and below the person whose job is enriched. Therefore, the enrichment of a job cannot be undertaken successfully without the participative involvement of the jobholder and all others (line, staff, and union) who would be affected by the enrichment of the job.

Task force approach. The jobholder approach can be amplified into a task force effort by having job incumbents, their supervisors, and union leaders work together on the exercises de-

Figure 9. Goal-oriented relationship between foreman and operator.

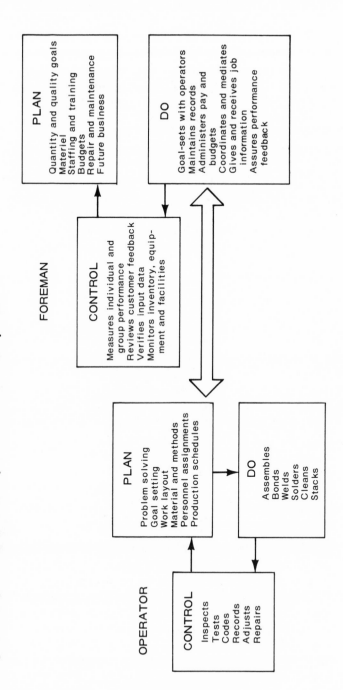

scribed in Figures 7 and 8. The success of this approach, of course, depends on the quality of the relationships of those involved in the process. People in effective work groups conditioned by experience in Work Simplification encounter little difficulty in attaining the relationship depicted in Figure 9.

Sometimes the most natural (and hence the most effective) task force approach to creating a whole job is through the problem-solving, goal-setting procedure which is, in effect, a group approach to Work Simplification. Here the focus is not on the job itself, but rather on the solution of a customer problem or on the attainment of a company goal. For example, the unselfconscious involvement of store managers, department heads, cashiers, clerk packers, and customers of a Canadian supermarket resulted in the expansion of a clerk-packer's menial job to the whole job depicted in Figure 10.

The consequence of the problem-solving, goal-setting approach is not only an opportunity to manage a job. More importantly, the widespread application of this process in the Canadian food chain resulted in a competitive advantage to the organization which increased job security and promotional opportunity for most members of the workforce. Hence, to the extent that clerk-packers realized both financial and psychological benefits from their new role, they were in a real sense working for themselves in the supermarket.

Management approach. In some circumstances, it is necessary for managers to design or redesign the jobs of subordinates without the involvement of the persons in those jobs. For example, in planning a new factory or office in preparation for expansion, long before job incumbents are on the payroll, managers may wish to design facilities, systems, and processes to provide meaningful roles for the people to be hired in the future. A manager in this situation should identify and indoctrinate his managerial people as early as possible in order to incorporate their ideas in, and evoke their commitment to, meaningful work strategies. Hence, a factory manager would involve all managerial people available in an orientation session on the philosophy, goals, and techniques of industrial democracy. As a minimum requirement, this training program should include the plant manager himself, the

124

Figure 10. Clerk-packer as manager.

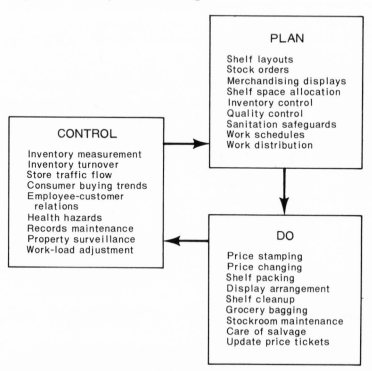

personnel director, plant engineer, manufacturing manager, the people who will be in charge of industrial engineering, quality control, EDP, maintenance, and as many as possible of the first- and second-level supervisors. If at this stage the unions which will represent members of the bargaining units are known, union leaders should be included in job enrichment planning. Whether or not a union will represent employees in the new facility cannot, of course, be predetermined by upper management but can only be determined by the employees themselves.

It would be ideal, of course, to include all supervisory people in this advance planning phase but, in practice, new operations usually begin with skeleton staffs and add supervisors as plans are implemented. As new staff are added, they should be selected for their compatibility with the prescribed managerial philosophy, and fully oriented before assuming their supervisory roles.

One of the tangible achievements of this skeleton staff is the actual definition of several plan-do-control models based on concepts and procedures reflected in Figures 1 through 8. Before crystallizing managerial jobs, initial effort should be devoted to designing key wage-roll jobs in terms of plan-do-control. Enriching the operators' jobs usually results in the enrichment of supervisors' jobs also, as is shown by comparing the content of the foreman's job in Figure 9 and his job in Figure 5.

Thus, the plan-do-control model administered in the workplace appeals to a number of human needs, one of which is the sense of autonomy which characterizes the self-employed entrepreneur. Such a person is thinking and acting like a manager, and is said to have a joint stake in the success of the organization.

Human Energy for Innovation

Glenn R. Cowan

Glenn R. Cowan's pervading interest in creativity has been displayed throughout his varied career in education, engineering, and management consulting. Since 1954 he has served as consultant, instructor, and course dean of the Creative Problem Solving Institute at the State University of New York at Buffalo. Mr. Cowan was chairman of the steering committee and first president of the Improvement Institute.

INTRODUCTION

All individuals are blessed (or plagued) with an energy for innovation. Mankind's creative being in itself cannot be qualified as "good" or "bad," but it must be exercised well—or great harm will come to the self. The human being must create order out of chaos or he must create chaos out of order so the process of rebirth can be repeated. This is the universal process of growth of which man is a part. He was so created by his maker.

Managers must sooner or later face the necessity of managing under conditions of change, yet few are "managers of change." These few understand the powerful force of the energy for innovation among their people. They understand and manage the *processes* of change so that this energy becomes a productive force rather than a destructive one.

The following series of letters is a real-life attempt to encourage a managing director to manage the processes of change and thus to harness the human energy to develop the growth potential which existed. His company in New Zealand had been suffering from several undesirable conditions:

> It had a troublesome union. The union leadership was strong and smart.
> It had experienced, for many years, a strongly dictatorial but extremely paternalistic management.
> It had a first-line supervisory force that had experienced many years of simply "carrying out orders."
> Its profit picture showed a rapid decline.
> Its market share was falling.
> Employees were of high caliber with high seniority.

I had previously prepared a step-by-step procedural system for an improvement project program for this plant. It had been assigned to a staff assistant—and nothing happened. I realized then that the top management at that company needed to understand and appreciate the background for the system before anything could take place—hence, my letters to "John."

Dear John: August 6, 1974

Your organization is like any other organization that sets out with an objective to improve its effectiveness: The barriers seem immovable, and it seems impossible to find the answer to the simple question, "What is wrong?" The simple fact is that there is nothing wrong. That type of question and the philosophy behind it cannot produce change; rather, it does just the opposite. Let me explain.

Change and innovation produce improvement. Improvement cannot take place without them. The rate of change therefore is a determinant of the rate of improvement. Understandably, change increases the chance of something "going wrong." The question "What is wrong?" is useless and unanswerable. To live with change, your organization must develop a tolerance for doing something wrong—for something to be out of control. "Tight ship" organizations—which are resistant to change—abhor situations that are not under control at all times.

This brings us to another phenomenon. When an organization needs to change, when there is clear evidence that something must be done, the natural organizational response is to tighten the reigns of control. This can be done in a number of ways. One is to pass the reigns of control higher up in the hierarchy of the organization. Another is to impose tighter control systems within the organization, or to replace the managers with others of a tighter sort.

This defensive mechanism of the organization drives the processes of change further and further into the background. Changes, of course, may take place, but these changes will be heavily imposed. The spirit of change and the internal human energy for innovation will be depressed. A clear case of "too much management—too little change" (as Leo Moore expressed it) will most certainly exist.

Your organization needs an agency that serves as the ombudsman of change. Such an agency should have more than a temporary status. It needs to be more than a task force venture. Otherwise, employees will assume it to be just another one of the "firefighting" techniques under a new name. It must be distinguishable from any other of the "control devices" established under periods of crisis.

Some questions come to mind. What are the components of change? What new managerial techniques must be developed and instituted if the human energy for change is to be utilized?

First, let us examine the components of change. There are two useful categories of change. The first type is those changes largely developed outside of the affected organization. These are generally new or revised equipment and tools, processes or material, specifications or product designs. In general they are the technological changes.

The change function to be managed in these changes is the *acceptance* of change. This is generally not too difficult to manage because the typical control techniques of an organization, in general, can effectively implement them. Trial and error activities are not involved in a primary way. There are comparatively few problems and disruptions to the regular order of things. The task is simply to fit the new into the old habits or systems.

The second type of change is the one that is internally developed. For convenience, we shall call the process "innovation." Innovation is rather commonly equated with invention—it is used to name the "thing" that results, rather than the change process in its entirety. But by innovation I refer to the *total change process,* the creative process of change.

After all, if changes are needed to accomplish your organizational objective, then you must consider the *process* of change itself. A workable change process must be developed within the organization. It cannot be assumed to come into existence just because the need for it is evident. It must be willfully created.

Sincerely,

Glenn R. Cowan

Dear John: August 17, 1974

In my last letter to you I encouraged you to consider some system or process to initiate change by the people in your organization. You replied that even the changes needed to make possible the managing of the change process seem to be resisted.

This could very well be. If so, you should not be discouraged. It only shows your organization as it is now cannot tolerate the change process. Ironically, the organization most needing to change is the one least able to do it. Conversely, I have discovered through the years that organizations least needing a system for managing change are those that most readily and successfully generate such a system.

It might be helpful to give a little thought to the phenomenon called "resistance to change."

We have made certain discoveries about resistance to change. Early researchers in the field were naturally more concerned with acceptance of change. It was discovered that acceptance was increased and resistance decreased as the degree of being "in on" or "in the know" regarding change was increased. The "Hawthorne Studies" gave some clues to this.

More recently, the notion that people do not resist change as much as they resist being changed became a guiding philosophy. The management groups studying under A. H. Mogensen at Lake Placid, New York, were prime practitioners of this philosophy.

I suggest to you even more positively that there is an inherent human energy for innovation, which should not be thwarted. Perhaps the stronger an apparent resistance to change (any change) exists, the more likely that there also exists a thwarted energy for making or initiating change by many people in the organization. In other words, people who are not allowed to make changes themselves are the strongest to resist having changes imposed upon them. Psychologically this notion makes sense from a number of angles.

Let us look at this possibility. Assume that a human energy for innovation does exist. Assume that the energy to seek change is a natural response to some stimuli. Human dissatisfaction normally results in an urge to change something, the impetus to try some new course of action.

The advertising profession, which studies human motivation, works on these assumptions. Day by day, I am bombarded by the admen on TV with constant reminders of my little dissatisfactions. They are playing on my urge to change, my natural way of reacting to dissatisfactions. The adman expects me to move. He is also on hand with an attractively presented alternative. He depends on me to initiate a change. He cannot impose change upon me but he can gamble with assurance upon my human energy for innovation. He has two goals:

131

1. The arousal of my dissatisfaction, thus triggering my energy to change.
2. The appeal to my logic and reason to satisfy this energy release need by buying his product.

One thing he does know—once I am fully dissatisfied I will do something!

I do not know whether my arguments are convincing or not on this point. Assuming that energy for innovation does exist, let's see where it could lead us.

If you are to institute change, then, the first order of business might be to find out who is dissatisfied, or shows signs of dissatisfaction. What are the things they are dissatisfied about? (It is more positive to ask directly, "What are your concerns?") But, however it is determined, it is important to find out the areas and directions of potential energy for change. This investigation may then give the starting point of the change process. In view of the previous experience of meeting resistance, I suggest that you consider it.

Sincerely,

Glenn R. Cowan

Dear John: August 28, 1974

In your last letter reporting your attempts to uncover dissatisfactions as a starting point for change, you indicated that the results were inconclusive and not very illuminating.

However, I did find some clues to the situation during my last visit to your plant. As you know, I met with some of your people in discussion sessions.

From this small sample of your supervisors' feelings about their jobs, one thing is clear: Not very much is happening—changes do not originate in that group. The potential for change does exist, but a managed program for the nurture and care of innovative energies is needed. Your first-line supervisors are potential participants in such a venture. This is not to say either that they should be first to establish it or that they should be the only ones to engage in it.

The inconclusive results of your study of the situation and the results of the questionnaire indicate that some top management demonstration is needed to give impetus to the effort. The supervisors are not entirely confident that the changes which they visualize are really wanted and welcome. Perhaps old customs or practices of management by control from the top stand in the way.

The logjam must be broken. With initiation of change at a zero level, of course, acceptance of change is at a low level, too. It should be pointed out that compliance with change is not the same as acceptance of change.

Sincerely,

Glenn R. Cowan

September 10, 1974

Dear John:

Since I last discussed the topic of an organized change function for your organization, I've realized that you might have reached a danger point if you're now convinced that an organized change agency is a necessity. The danger is that, due to the urgency that you may now feel, you would try to force the agency into effect by managerial edict.

This is a delicate situation. First, from your management position at the very top of the hierarchy, your wish may be a command. Care must be taken as to how you proceed. Second, the human energy for innovation is an expression of man's creative being—it cannot be forced. Even though this energy exists and needs expression, it can easily be frustrated and diverted into unwanted channels. Examples of this diverted activity are excessive union activity, ingenious soldiering on the job, and busywork. Innovation must be self-directed. Channeling it becomes the delicate part of the task at hand.

Let me give you an example of an instance that illustrates this point quite well. The personnel in a plant had a history of neither changing nor questioning existing situations. In a series of meetings with a few supervisors, however, it became evident that they did have dissatisfactions. They did see possibilities of change and improvement. They also felt voiceless in the matter. This small group of supervisors agreed to act as a committee to draft a proposal which would give them a means to communicate and to act upon their ideas for improvement. I advised this group.

The next step of this committee was to have a series of meetings with all supervisors. Some changes in the committee's proposal were made as a result. This being done, the committee was urged by the entire group to present the idea to the management.

They did so. Some managers showed some reluctance. Others were considerably against the notion, but the final word was to give their approval to the supervisors to undertake the program.

Some innovations in plant operations were generated through this system, the original impetus coming, for the most part, from the original committee. Activity began to build slowly. It seemed that it could become an important force for change and improvement in this plant. The plant manager now became very interested in the activity. Previously he had only accepted it. He could see a good thing coming. He decided to make it "his" program. The first visual move was to rename it. This "take-over" by the plant manager was enough to dampen the enthusiasm that had been voluntary. The drive initiated by the committee eased off. The supervisors no longer expressed their energy for innovation, at least in the positive manner in which they had started.

Channeling this energy, then, is a delicate thing—so delicate, in fact, that few organizations have shown the ability to do it: Texas Instruments Company is one in the United States. A number of manufacturing plants in Japan appear to have done it, too. They involve not only supervisors, managers, and staff personnel, but production workers as well. I have talked to plant managers from Japan about this involvement of the worker group in the process of change in the plant. The responses were indirect but, nevertheless, very revealing.

I asked one plant manager from Japan, "Do Japanese workers and production supervisors get together to discuss and work out changes that will improve production and quality?" He answered, "Yes, it is only natural to do that." "But," I said, "I read that the government sponsored the idea that once each week workers must discuss the quality of their work and product. Do you really meet once a week to do that?" "Yes," he said, "but much more often." I learned by considerable reading about the Japanese plant activity that the first volunteer worker groups were concerned with work quality and product quality. However, now improvements in the work and work methods are also devised by these work center meetings.

They must be concerned with more than quality. Their productivity has been favorably affected. I have data on a number of Japanese plants regarding their output. [See Figure 1 comparing indices of productivity improvements with similar plants in

Figure I. Comparative productivity index chart for associate plants 1973-1974.

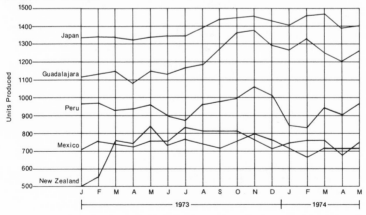

135

various other countries of the world. Eds.] The Japanese rate of change in productivity during 1973 was about 12 percent greater, while United States government figures peg the U.S. industry productivity change at 2.4 percent per year.

On this same basis, the August 24, 1974, issue of *Business Week* reports that "Texas Instruments Company has a productivity improvement rate of 14 percent per year as compared to 2.4 percent for the remainder of U.S. industry."[1] All the personnel of both the Texas Instruments Company plants and the Japanese plants have direct involvement in the processes of innovation. The Texas Instruments Company employs a number of techniques described very aptly by Dr. Scott Myers.[2] Some insight into Japanese techniques is provided in the following excerpts from a report by Kaoru Ishikawa of the University of Tokyo.[3] Mr. Ishikawa describes growth, development, and the activities of the QC Circle movement in Japanese industry. A QC Circle is a group of all workers led by a foreman or supervisor at its nucleus and organized in each workshop or work unit. Some references below relate to the management role.

Formation and activity of the QC Circle is spontaneous in that it is not forced on employees by will or regulation of the company. People in the circle take an initiative in viewing problems in the workshop, tackling them, and discovering the ways and means of solving them, and make breakthroughs from the management interest point of view. They are willing to assume a firm, positive attitude toward works of their responsibility and strive to achieve the goal as set by the company in their own free will.

Companies having difficulty in the movement are invariably

---

[1] "Texas Instruments: Pushing Hard into the Consumer Markets," *Business Week,* August 24, 1974, pp. 39–42.

[2] Dr. Scott Myers, "Who Are Your Motivated Workers?" *Harvard Business Review,* January-February 1964.

[3] Quotations from an article written by Kaoru Ishikawa in the *JUSE* (*Journal of Japan Union of Science and Engineers*), Vol. 16, no. 3, 1969.

ones which forced the idea on the production workers in the *introductory period* of the QC Circle operation, giving little or no regard for their free will.

Later in his report, Mr. Ishikawa notes that constant attention must be paid to the QC Circle activity: "However, a caution must be exercised that the management or management staff people do not make too much intervention with or control over the activity of the QC Circles. They should refrain from telling the circles what to do or what not to do, which tends to discourage their spontaneous wish of achieving something worthy of doing."

Mr. Ishikawa does go on to point out that after QC Circle activities are well established and widespread in scope throughout any one plant, stronger managerial guidance is not only acceptable by the various circles but it is expected and even requested. This article by Mr. Ishikawa quite specifically describes the delicate nature of this voluntary activity.

Sincerely,

Glenn R. Cowan

CONCLUSION

The latent energy for innovation is found in human need and longing for new experience and growth. It is perhaps best expressed by Dr. Abraham Maslow. (For a synthesis of Maslow, see *The Third Force* by Frank Goble, New York: Grossman, 1970.) Dr. Maslow's observations indicate that even though the energy for innovation does exist in man, it tends to be diverted or submerged in most people after the early childhood years. Therefore, it is not enough merely to provide situations conducive to growth through innovation. The exercise of this energy must be learned, or relearned, by adults. Adults cannot return to childhood to learn some patterns for utilizing innovative behavior. Some structured behavioral sequences must be practiced and learned in order for most adults to handle randomness, spontaneity, imagination, uninhibitedness, sensitivity, free association, intuitive perception, and similar behavioral attributes which enhance the use of innovative energies.

In this regard it might be helpful to read carefully Dr. Jean Piaget's *To Understand Is To Invent*. According to Dr. Piaget, innovation and mental growth are inseparable, if not synonymous. Although Dr. Piaget is referring to the learning situation of the child and youth, his findings pertain to our situation as we help adults in our organizations to relearn, through a guided experience, a pattern for innovative behavior. Such learned patterns seem to be necessary for those whose innovative energies have atrophied through neglect and nonuse. This is the "oversight" that is the emphasis of this book and the thrust of the Improvement Institute, under whose auspices this volume originated. Clearly our challenge is to invent a suitable "unmanagement device" that transcends management by control and affects the optimizing of the *human energy* for innovation. We seem to be adept at managing and using man's analytical abilities. Can we be equally adept at releasing and utilizing his *energy for innovation and change?*

The Improvement Program

A Comparison of SYI with the Team Approach

Richard F. Weaver

Richard F. Weaver is vice-president and director of the Work Factor Foundation. His broad background includes experience in industrial relations and industrial engineering. A former trustee and president of the Improvement Institute, Mr. Weaver is chairman of the International Advisory Board. He is also director of the Management Institute, Glassboro State College.

All improvement programs, regardless of title, administration, or coverage, seek to attain a single objective—constructive change.

Improvement programs seek to involve people in the ideation and implementation of improvements. Ideation encompasses problem definition, data gathering, analysis, and solution development. Implementation is the process of bringing the solution into being.

Two general types of improvement program (with almost infinite minor variations) are in effect in the United States and other industrialized countries. The Submit Your Idea Program, SYI, the oldest and most prevalent type, concentrates upon the idea-

139

tion phase of improvement while the second type, Teams, emphasizes implementation. The two employ differing methodology to attain their objectives.

SYI

In its original form, this program is typified by the suggestion program. The major premise, rooted in the invention-patent history of this country, envisions an original, creative idea as the basis for obtaining improvement. That this premise is suspect, antiquated, and—in most cases—fallacious, is illustrated by the fact that it takes entire research organizations dedicated to providing ideas and data to produce useable ideas, while SYI assumes that any employee can do it alone.

Creativity research generally concludes that assimilative processes—the forcing of different relationships or the application of known or conceived processes in a different functional area—constitute creativity. Do these processes result in original ideas? Is there such a thing as an original idea? SYI claims the answer to both questions is yes. As a source of improvement, SYI programs claim millions of dollars in savings each year.

Let us consider the functioning of SYI. In general, three distinct persons or groups are involved in the system: the submitter, the administrator, and the investigator-implementer. Their functions in SYI are summarized in Figure 1.

The submitter is responsible for presenting an "original idea," usually consisting of a problem statement and a solution. His idea is presented in writing, usually a paragraph or less, and the submitter's identity is secret except to the administrator. Motivation for the submitter is ascribed to the potential monetary reward, typically 10 to 15 percent of the first-year savings.

The administrator is charged with the responsibility of collecting and processing the written suggestions. After recording the submitter's identity, the administrator assigns the suggestion to the individual or area representative who would be most affected

Figure I. Operation of a "Submit Your Idea" (SYI) program.

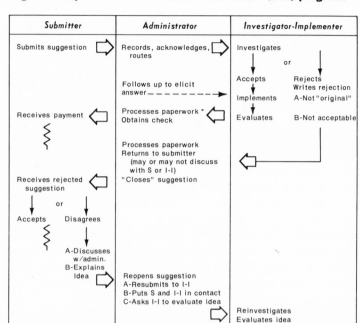

by the proposed improvement. Motivation for the administrator is through the normal promotion and evaluation processes.

The investigator-implementer is charged with interpreting the written statement of the problem and the proposed solution. He evaluates the suggestion in light of his knowledge of the circumstances and, if the suggestion is acceptable, performs the necessary steps to implement the improvement.

141

As the investigator-implementer is frequently responsible for the work to be improved by the suggestion, his motivation and responses are complex. Examination of the emotive interaction of the investigator-implementer and the "system" may readily explain why 75 to 80 percent of all suggestions are initially rejected. It will also help in isolating several causes of the failure of the investigator-implementer to be a strong supporter of the SYI improvement program.

Since the investigator-implementer in most SYI programs should be the person most knowledgeable to judge the merit of the suggestion, he most often is the person already charged with the responsibility for the particular activity (function, job, task) which the suggestion seeks to improve.

Confronted by a written, usually bluntly stated suggestion from an *unknown source,* the average investigator-implementer tends to react defensively. Although well meant, the suggestion is often viewed as a criticism of his performance or his personal value. The weaker the ego and the greater the pride in job performance, the more intense the emotional response will be. Relatively few people achieve the level of security needed to accept a valid criticism or suggestion without feeling personally criticized or faulted.

The natural reaction to criticism is negative. If the idea is good and significant, the investigator-implementer may have feelings of inadequacy or loss of face because he did not think of it first; or, he may feel hostile as a result of the perceived ego threat and insecurity. If the idea has already been tried, he may feel that he is wasting precious time evaluating an idea that has already been thoroughly analyzed.

Furthermore, the investigator-implementer has to overcome the communications barrier inherent in the briefly written suggestion. Technical writers spend pages attempting to provide problem statements. Books are written to classify and provide solutions. Yet a suggestion, in a brief paragraph, usually in longhand and often illegible, attempts to describe a problem and tender a solution for investigation. Still another communication problem arises: The problem as stated by the submitter is often understood differently by the investigator-implementer. To him it may be obvious that only a small portion of the problem is perceived by the submitter. Hence, the solution as presented and interpreted will not solve the problem and the suggestion is rejected. The suggestion is returned to the submitter through the administrator, and approximately 80 percent of the time this concludes the process.

How do the three persons or groups involved feel about the system after the suggestion is rejected?

Submitter. If the reasons for rejection are complete and clearly stated by the investigator, the submitter may be satisfied. In the majority of cases, however, he is not satisfied. Frequently he has waited months for an answer. If the suggestion is adapted, he may wait even longer for full implementation, evaluation, and payment. He is unaware of the difficulty the investigator had in reading and understanding the suggestion. The reasons for rejection are often incomplete. If rejected as not original, he may be reluctant to believe it was previously thought of or tried, even when he is confronted with documented evidence.

If the submitter doubts the integrity of the program ("nobody pays for half the ideas they get"; "people steal ideas"; "the program is designed to sucker people into making suggestions"), rejection or inadequate explanation will reinforce this bias. This results in subsequent refusal to submit. If he believes in the program but is dissatisfied with the answer, he may request that the administrator reopen the suggestion.

Administrator. Charged with "making the system perform," he is responsible for a certain number of suggestions submitted, processed, and adopted. He is caught between the impatience and dissatisfaction of the suggestor and the complaints and procrastination of the investigator-implementer. Unless the administrator and his supervisor understand the response patterns of the other personnel necessary to the program, the administrator may resort to these rationalizations: The submitter must be paid more to obtain his cooperation, the investigator is not being objective in the evaluation, or the investigator doesn't give suggestions the priority he should.

143

Investigator-implementer. As he sees SYI, he has nothing positive to gain and a series of frustrations to endure. He must overcome a communications barrier to attempt to interpret the suggestion. He may feel criticized. He must spend precious time to investigate and reply in writing to satisfy the administrator and the submitter. He becomes inundated with suggestions during special drives to meet the administrator's goals and receives negative reinforcement when he does not answer on time, completely, or correctly.

No more than half the suggestions adopted or implemented are processed to completion the first time through. These *do not* represent the largest savings. The "big savings" suggestions almost invariably follow the second phase of the SYI program—resubmission or reopening.

If the submitter is unhappy or aggressive enough, he will discuss his rejected suggestion with the administrator. He explains what he meant, how he saw the problem, and ramifications of his solution. The administrator may now discard the secret identity requirement and put the submitter and investigator-implementer into contact.

If the suggestion is not a complete, useable proposal, the investigator-implementer is requested to evaluate the *idea*. If the idea is not original, he must evaluate the possibility of the suggestion playing a role in the implementation of any portion of the improvement. A major SYI tenet is now discarded; the suggestion need not be original in order to be adopted, installed, and paid!

During this process, the investigator-implementer has provided up to 90 percent of the ideation and 100 percent of the implementation. The submitter receives the positive recognition, publicity, credit, and money!

Normal adoption rates in suggestion programs are 15 to 25 percent, and even successful suggesters are not completely satisfied. Although "inadequate payment" may be a source of discontent, more vocal criticism concerns payment for suggestions not used, incompletely adopted, or discontinued.

Discussions with employees in both large and small companies support the premise that they want to make a contribution, to see their contribution in action, and then, if it is of value, to receive the promised monetary reward. The submitter is told, "You are important, we want your ideas." He perceives, however, that he is ignored for a long period of time, his ideas are not investigated to his satisfaction, and responses are inadequate. How many of these frustrating experiences are needed to make sure that he no longer participates?

SYI certainly discourages participation in improvement programs, since it elicits negative responses from the majority of those involved. Were it not for the vested interest of those charged with program administration, more major modifications or discontinuations of the program would have occurred years ago. To attain improvement program objectives, there are much less tortuous and frustrating routes than the classic SYI program! Many modifications have been undertaken to improve the program, but the basic emphasis on individual payment for an original idea, secretly submitted, still consumes inordinate man-hours for the degree of improvement attained. In addition, two of three members of the system experience damaged attitudes toward all improvement efforts.

THE TEAM APPROACH

The Team Approach recognizes that implementation is the most important phase of the improvement process. An idea is useless unless something is done with it! The team concept is founded on the premise that improvement is part of everyone's job and that a vehicle for recognizing and reporting improvement efforts is necessary.

Unlike SYI, which emphasizes external problem solution as the source of improvement, the Team Approach emphasizes group ideation and implementation. Problems in the vested interest area of the team members are of prime concern, and all who are affected are invited to participate throughout in ideation and implementation. This creates positive attitudes toward im-

145

provement as each is fully involved in the entire improvement process.

Team members see improvement as a part of their jobs. They gain positive recognition for their efforts and benefits from the improvement. Because all involved in the problem participate in the solution, all the team members are committed to the improvement. All ramifications are explored, and related problems are tackled and solved. Performance goals are established and a continuing improvement effort is obtained instead of the one-shot approach of SYI. The average processing time from problem definition to solution implementation is about six weeks vs. six months processing time for SYI. Instead of the 25 percent participation in SYI, teams often average up to two completed projects per team member per month. Instead of writing, routing, and processing paperwork (the mill of SYI), only the project title is reported and progress noted; the completed team project requires about as much writing as the original submission of a suggestion. An annual adoption ratio of one per ten eligible employees is usually high for SYI; a project implementation ratio of one or two per each eligible employee is not unusual in the Team Approach.

The Team Approach is exemplified by the Management of Improvement, Methods Improvement, or Work Simplification Programs in many organizations. The objective of these programs is "to create a management philosophy providing a favorable climate which promotes, on a continuing basis and in an organized manner, the involvement of employees to participate in the ideation and implementation of improvement."

The statement of the objective recognizes that there are prerequisites necessary to establish and continue an effective improvement program—in effect the program must be important to more than the administrators. The program must be important to all participants—everyone has something to gain—and management must overtly demonstrate their support (by ensuring that time is made available, by asserting that problem solving is a way of life, and so on). The program must be the manager's program; administration becomes a collection-dispersion-consulting

146

function or an aid to the manager (unlike the SYI program in which the administrator attempts to elicit support).

The Three Phases of the Program

An effective improvement program utilizing the Team Approach consists of three phases plus feedback. Phase I, *appreciation,* involves top level management participation in 16 to 24 hours of discussion on philosophy, problem-solving techniques, tools and techniques, their role in the program, and projected cost in time and money and program benefits. Phase II, *education,* consists of 20 to 48 hours of training for subordinates preparing them for their role in Phase III, *application.*

In the application phase, teams may be structured vertically or horizontally. In large organizations, vertical teams of three to six employees are often formed within departments on a permanent basis. Large departments may have several teams; small departments, only one. A permanent team captain, responsible for meeting dates, notification, and reporting is appointed or elected. Departments with multiple teams usually have a department coordinator appointed. (Typical vertical team structure is illustrated in Figure 2.)

Figure 2. Typical vertical teams.

Engineering Team 1		Manufacturing Team 1		Manufacturing Team 2		Financial Team 1	
Manager	Team Captain	Superintendent	Team Captain	Superintendent	Team Captain	Manager	Team Captain
Engineer	Team Member	Supervisor	Team Member	Supervisor	Team Member	Accountant	Team Member
Engineer	Team Member	Supervisor	Team Member	Supervisor	Team Member	Accountant	Team Member
Engineer	Team Member	Supervisor	Team Member	Supervisor	Team Member	Accounting Clerk	Team Member
Engineering Technician	Team Member			Supervisor	Team Member	Accounting Clerk	Team Member
				Supervisor	Team Member		

In operation, team members serve as rotating captains conducting problem-solving meetings or parts of the meeting. When problems affect other departments or outside assistance is required, temporary team members are solicited to participate in problem definition-solution and to make commitments for implementation. (See Figure 3.)

Figure 3. Vertical team in action, project X.

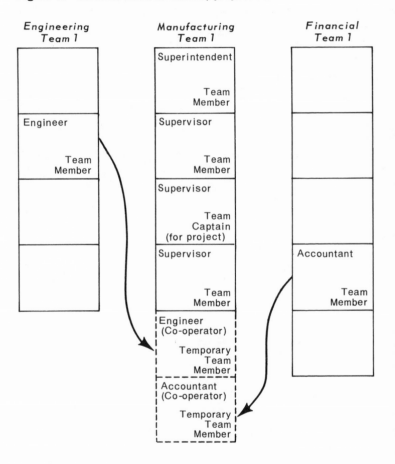

Vertical vs. Horizontal Teams

Vertical teams have the advantages of (1) support and reinforcement from their management; (2) closer proximity to the problem under consideration and hence a vested interest in faster solution implementation; (3) stronger and better rapport for any capital necessary for implementation; (4) continuing opportunities to attend meetings and devote time to fact-finding and solution implementation.

Horizontal teams are often used in smaller organizations. Such a team might be made up of a manufacturing supervisor, product engineer, industrial engineer, material control supervisor, and quality control supervisor. Such teams may be permanent but, more frequently, are formed for single projects (as a task force or project team). The horizontal team has the advantage of a wide range of viewpoints and perceptions which can be brought to bear on the problem. Also, problems of broader scope may be considered. These same advantages can be incorporated into vertical teams through the involvement and participation of "cooperators."

There are disadvantages to the horizontal team: (1) the team is formed for and considers only one problem vs. several problems on the vertical team docket; (2) membership participation is not consistent as the problem does not directly bear on team members' regular responsibilities vs. participation in vertical teams by affected personnel; and (3) several months are usually required before solution implementation is obtained vs. an average of six weeks.

The Administrator's Role

The administrator's role in the Team Approach is to provide training (Phase II); to collect, consolidate, and distribute reports of completed projects; to analyze projects and team performance for the managers; and to assure recognition in the form of dinners, certificates, distinctive awards, and publicity to be pre-

149

sented by the managers. He is a consultant to the managers and team members, providing ideas and advice on improving performance in the improvement process. He may assist in isolating potentially negative procedures and watch for degeneration of a team into competing or nonparticipating individuals. The program is *not* his program as in SYI, but the managers' and subordinates' program.

The administrator conducts a monthly meeting of team captains where completed projects are reported and current projects discussed to assure participation of all affected. Feedback is received which permits evaluation of team performance, needs, and desires. The administrator assures that projects are evaluated and points awarded, and attends committee meetings of top management where policy decisions affecting the improvement program are made.

The Role of Awards

The application phase of the improvement program provides an *external* vehicle for recognition and awards. It is external, because a special improvement program would not be necessary if improvement were really regarded as an important part of everyone's job; if promotion, awards, and other forms of recognition were adequately provided by managers; and if management programs designed to develop manpower, organization, and management were utilized. Local managers would know the kind and amount of recognition proper for each employee, and how recognition of one employee reflects on and is evaluated by every other employee. Employee performance would be measured not only on performance in vested areas but also on contribution to improvement. Since the existing awards and recognition of management and management development programs in general use are not perceived as adequate or helpful by the majority of managers and employees, the external vehicle provided in Phase III is extremely important.

150

Awards are an integral part of the Team Approach. Since the goal is to have everyone participate in improvement efforts, points are awarded for completed projects, not just for dollars saved. From my observations, in programs where dollars are the prime consideration, only those persons having control over dollar expenditure (such as manufacturing, engineering, and purchasing) actively participate. Others affected (the majority of salaried employees) do *not* participate. As a result, solutions are not implemented because the affected people necessary to implementation feel they have nothing to gain from the program.

In a program where implemented improvement is the goal, dollars are not excluded but are translated into points so that all can receive awards and all are encouraged to participate. Improvements are implemented; dollar savings are a byproduct. Cooperators receive points for their efforts, and points accrue to their teams without subtracting from the original team. As long as awards remain nominal and distinctive, competition for them works to further the improvement/implementation activities of the teams and their members. However, rewards are not to be made part of the competitive portion of the program. Rewards, through advancement, can and should be provided by the manager of the team members. But if recognition and awards assume the character of rewards or "payment" as in suggestion programs, competition between teams can be a deterrent to participation and involvement. Rewards can create a win-lose conflict to the advantage of a few teams and to the disadvantage of the total improvement program. Participants are then recognized for being "exceptional" rather than for doing what everyone should be doing, trying to improve.

Properly coordinated, organization development and improvement program goals are compatible. Monthly feedback from the administrator of opened/implemented projects provides data on progress toward organization goals. Additional benefits accrue to the organization and to participating personnel if there is recognition of who the managers of improvement are, or who the problem-recognition and problem-solving personnel are, and if this is

151

conceived as a criterion for advancement and merit increases.

As conceptualized, a merit increase program would like performance to be closely followed by reward. In reality, what is called the merit increase program is usually a vehicle for "time-in-grade" review. As perceived and reinforced, most operating management believes that performance in vested areas is more important than the ability to manage. The ability to manage, to recognize and work on problems, is easily discerned by observing operations under the Team Approach.

Ample opportunities are provided for individual evaluation in the roles of project team captain and team member. If the management of improvement is a valid indication of managerial skill, the Team Approach should provide an objective source of evaluative data, easily assimilated as part of the criteria for advancement and merit increases.

Human emotions are not disregarded in the Team Approach, but facets of program operation are designed to alleviate emotional factors and to overcome dysfunctional responses. Many people have seen improvement programs fade for lack of management commitment ("apply the panacea and reap the benefits, but don't interfere with my regular work"). These tend to participate halfheartedly in team activity until their managers overtly demonstrate that participation is really valued—that is, when the manager shows consistent concern for the number of projects implemented, team meeting attendance, scope of projects, and thoroughness of problem-solution performance against goals. In general, the manager must convey the feeling that improvement is part of *everyone's* job.

The working rapport, problem-solving techniques and methodology, and the philosophy of the Team Approach should be inherent in any organization. Its success is vested in the managers. When improvement truly becomes a part of everyone's job; when recognition, promotion, merit increases, and awards are based on improvement—and *everyone* perceives this to be so—then the external improvement program will be ready for assimilation.

Benefits of the Team Approach

Although significant improvements and savings are ascribed to the Team Approach, the biggest benefit derived is the lessening of hostility and distrust among affected employees during the problem perception-solution process. Since all affected play a role in the process, assigning blame is not of prime importance; rather, the cause and the common solution and improvement become the basis of the improvement process. Daily relations between peers and departments improve dramatically. Artificial kingdom boundaries are lowered and even eliminated. One plant manager stated that even with annual savings of more than a million dollars, the greatest asset of the Team Approach is the improvement in day-to-day operations between employees and departments.

Instead of a program which concentrates on telling someone how to improve his activity, team members can actively eliminate their problems within the team framework. Team members, in addition to recognition and awards, have the advantage of being recipients and users of the implemented improvement—of working in an environment of their own design. Affected departments can be assured by including cooperators in the process so that elimination of one problem does not create a problem in another department. An overall attitude of mature responsibility is created. The problem becomes "ours" instead of "yours." The successful team is able to find larger interrelations between functions, and can tackle large, location-wide problems resulting in permanent improvement and important dollar savings. In fact, division-wide projects can grow out of what started as a local team project if all levels of management are made cognizant of possible improvement and are committed to the Team Approach.

In organizations where the Team Approach is used with hourly employees, the same results are achieved, even if employees are eligible for suggestion awards. They often become reluctant to write up their suggestions: whatever their level in the organization, employees want participation and involvement and like to see their improvements implemented.

The overall concepts of improvement management should profit from years of social and behavioral research and from practical experience. Antiquated techniques and programs must give way to new ones which recognize that the needs and wants of employees must coincide with organization goals. Management must move from programs which attempt to manipulate employees to programs which motivate. One excellent beginning is a movement from SYI to Teams and the establishment of the Team Approach for *all* people in business, organization, or plant.

Deliberate Methods Change

Its Concepts and Application

Arthur Spinanger

Arthur Spinanger, president of Spinanger Methods (Cincinnati, Ohio), developed the Methods Change program at Procter & Gamble, a program which yields more than $100 million in savings before taxes annually. He has published numerous articles on Work Simplification and materials handling.

The intent of this chapter on deliberate methods change is to give the reader a fuller and perhaps new perspective on methods change. In this perspective the reader will gain an appreciation of the difference between the usual "improvement or cost-reduction approach" with relatively limited results and the totally encompassing deliberate methods change with much greater benefits. The perspective on deliberate methods change will be obtained through views concentrating on first the concepts and then their application.

"PREVIEW" SUMMARY

A methods change program is a planned approach for making better things happen—*sooner*. It is an approach utilizing deliberate methods change concepts by which *every person would participate* in organized teams in any area of operation to attain specific self-set goals, individual and group growth, and achievement and job satisfaction.

In industry, a key goal is usually to increase profits. In other organizations, the goal may be something other than profits. For example, in hospital work it could be to expedite the patient's recovery or to reduce costs for the patient. In community welfare work, the goal may be to increase the benefits for the same cost or reduce the cost of the benefit while attaining the desired results.

Unlike most other approaches, the application of deliberate methods change is in no way a criticism—even implied—of the present method. Any method can deliberately be *changed* for the better—even when the operation is perfectly done. A methods program should *not* be viewed as *only* cost reduction. The total gains, especially the human ones, are far broader than that.

The attainment of these gains is helped considerably by the trained use of especially developed tools, all in the form of *unique* types of questions. By the organized use of these questioning approaches, which are simple to learn and simple to apply, almost any person—with or without experience in his or her area of responsibility—can effectively produce results meeting specific self-set goals. Thus, a methods change program provides for individual and group growth and meaningful achievements and job satisfaction. It is compatible with both personal and company objectives.

CONCEPTS

Deliberate methods change is *change for gain*—not a change for the sake of change. If no gain can be expected, then no change is made. The gain can be in anything: money, time, quality, health, or productivity. For example—in broad terms—an industry might make a methods change that produces an instant

156

gain in profits far beyond that obtained by a likely increase in sales in the same time.

In the environmental area, methods changes might be made to reduce pollution concentration in the air, water, or soil. In the health field, methods changes might be made to expedite the patient's recovery from an illness. Or a change might be made in the way of living to gain better mental and physical health—as by regularly performing simple light muscular motions to improve blood circulation. In the arts, the gain may be a change in the notes, words, or color to create a beautiful new song, book, poem, or painting.

But the most unique thing about this change for gain is that it is *deliberate*. Deliberate does *not* mean that the change is due to chance, an advantageous opportunity, or a critical problem needing correction. Deliberate does mean that the change is planned or brought about because of a commitment to do it.

A second unique thing about deliberate change is that it could be planned in any area of operation, whether the operation is faulty or perfect, whether the operation's intent is not met or met, whether the situation is a problem or not a problem. This latter point—that deliberate change applies to *any* area of operation—opens up the full potential of gain possibilities. Under the typical cost-reduction, problem-solving, or improvement approach, for example, most companies or organizations usually concentrate their actions on situations with high costs, disrupting problems, or poor or low efficiencies. When companies and organizations concentrate their actions on this type of situation, they are working mainly in areas having undesired results. With this concentration it is likely that they would not devote as much attention to areas with satisfactory results. It would be natural to ask, "And why should they?"

But in a successful company there are more things right than wrong. Thus, when a company devotes its main effort to things that are wrong, it is working on the *smaller* part of its business. It can easily miss greater opportunities for change because the larger part of its business is in the areas where things are done right. Of course, critical problems should be given attention—serious problems uncorrected could kill a company or organization. However, the gains from correcting the problems must be judged against the continuous new *added* gains from changing things, even if they are perfectly done. Non-problem areas—the ones usually not studied—are especially subject to deliberate change. A key characteristic of deliberate change is seen in a statement on its philosophy. It is a philosophy for making better things happen—sooner. And a key word in this philosophy is the word sooner.

A way of better appreciating this point may be seen through the diagram in Figure 1. The diagram is called "Situation 1 4 2 3." Assume that the left part of the main horizontal line, labeled 1, represents any initial situation. An initial situation could be anything—a *level* of cost, quality, safety, efficiency, profit, health, or productivity. What occurs at point 2 is that some outside source offers a new way of doing things, a new device, or a new material that could improve the situation. If the new way is adopted, then the situation becomes better than the initial one. Such advancements, when they occur, would be welcomed, of course.

Moving along the main horizontal line again to point 3, we see that when a problem occurs and is not instantly corrected, the level of the situation drops to a lower point. This lower level con-

Figure I. "Situation I423."

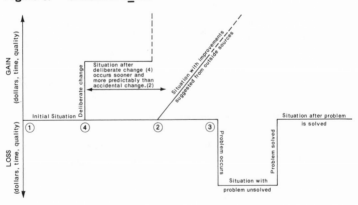

158

tinues until the problem is solved. The situation then returns (usually) to its initial value. The essential idea is that the *restored* level is not an improvement over the *initial* level. In other words, while the problem is corrected and a gain has been effected over the *unresolved* situation (below the starting line), no gain has been effected when compared to the initial value before the problem occurred. And certainly the situation after the problem is not as good as the situation 2 that has adopted a newly available change.

In a world of severe competition or damaging inflation, it is not enough to make "improvements" with zero gain. The degree of effort, time, and cost spent on this form of situation change (zero improvement) should be matched against the return brought about by "above-the-line" advancements. In both situations 2 and 3, there is one thing in common: neither is predictable—with respect to time or magnitude. And this brings us to situation 4—*deliberate change.*

In contrast to situations 2 and 3, results produced by deliberate change are largely predictable—and lend themselves to goal setting. Deliberate change produces a result that may be similar to but more predictable and sooner than situation 2, which is controlled by someone else's timetable. Deliberate change, situation 4, is far superior to situation 3, which does not advance beyond its original level after the problem is solved. Thus, to summarize, "Situation 1 4 2 3" gives us a perspective comparing the main characteristics of the various major ways of making changes.

In methods thinking we know that *any* operation can be changed to *any* extent at *any* time by *any* person because methods thinking has a power generated through two sources: an *attitude,* made strong by full belief and acceptance of deliberate change principles; and a *skill,* through use of unique questioning tools requiring the effective involvement of trained personnel. With deliberate-change thinking, it is not necessary to wait until a new method developed by someone else becomes available. Deliberate change is making changes *now*—not *waiting* for things to happen.

Every person is truly a manager when he or she responsibly participates in the changes, especially those concerning his or her own work. Deliberate-change successes compound themselves because they generate an ever-widening wave of enthusiasm brought about by the joy of genuine job satisfactions. People truly enjoy methods change when they originate the change themselves and feel they are meeting the challenge uniquely and successfully. When the power of people involvement is used on a *continual* basis (and not only on an emergency basis, as some cost-reduction programs are), the resulting gains grow enormously through reinforced experience.

For with constant deliberate change, the degree of change is not limited. From a cost-reduction standpoint alone, the savings potential is the full existing cost—because perfection is no barrier to change. Thus, as a battle cry, we can say, "Never consider any item of cost necessary"—and proceed to change for gain. When done on a large enough scale, such new methods will deflate inflationary conditions. We need only a way to apply these concepts.

APPLICATION

While concepts or a way of thinking form the basis on which action plans can be developed, for most effective application there needs to be a *vehicle* to carry out the action plans. For deliberate-change thinking such a vehicle is the methods change program. This is a program built on several of the unique characteristics of deliberate methods change. While all of the characteristics are firm supports of the program, three key members combine to form a natural medium that sustains the others. These three are *teams, goals,* and *recognition*—a team-goal approach supported by positive recognition.

The Team-Goal Approach

Briefly, under the team-goal approach, teams are composed of around five to eight people, usually drawn from one geographic

160

area. The teams may at first be only from management, but in the complete plan every employee can participate. Each team has a captain, and works on methods projects usually of their own selection.

With the goal emphasis, the highly desired advantages of establishing self-set targets and then aiming for them are secured. The goals (in industry, usually an annual dollar goal) would be self-set on the basis of how good each team thinks it is; and a promise to the company. With the attainment of the goal, recognition—usually nonmonetary but always appropriate to the occasion and the people involved—becomes a deserved meaningful highlight. With recognition, people completing successful methods changes gain a great feeling of achievement and responsibility, grow in knowledge, and gain opportunity for advancement. This leads to job satisfaction and a greater part in the decision making about their work.

Changes for Gain and Increasing Profits

Gains can be a desirable change in money, time, quality, or safety—many things. In industry, this desired change would usually include profits as one of the key goals. Let's look at such changes whose goal is to increase profits.

In its simplest terms, profit is the positive difference between receipts and expenses. According to the expression

$$\text{profits} = \text{receipts} - \text{expenses}$$

profits can be changed by changing receipts and/or expenses. More specifically, profits can be increased if expenses are reduced (assuming receipts remain constant). This kind of change to increase profits is usually called cost reduction.

Obviously, profits can also be increased if receipts or income are increased (assuming expenses remain constant). This kind of change to increase profits usually results from increased sales. Increased sales would be brought about by more effective advertising, increased sales effort, new products, or new product qualities which the customers desire at the same price as the old.

161

Increased profits can also occur when expenses are increased, provided the new expenses bring back a still higher receipt. For example, the addition of an air conditioner to an automobile increased the price of the car but also greatly increased the sales volume to people wanting a car with such an advantage.

Increased profits can occur when receipts are decreased, provided the expenses are decreased even more. For example, discontinuing a marginal profit product may decrease sales slightly but decrease expenses even more.

Of course, increased profits can occur with the best combination of these: increased receipts and decreased expenses. A recent news item may be used to demonstrate this point. In Germany, and more recently in the United States, apple-orchard growers were faced with both limited crops and increasing operating costs—a double blow to making a reasonable profit. Installation of cost-reducing steps in farming, better growing practices, and more efficient distribution methods were not enough to make a fair profit. Then a German farmer tried *renting* his several thousand apple trees to individual apple consumers from nearby cities.

All the usual pruning, cultivating, propping, spraying, harvesting, and transporting are done by the renters who can see and enjoy the fruits of their efforts. The farmer supplies only the easily used orchard equipment—and only frowns on any chopping. The result? At the rental rate of $8 per year per tree in Germany (in the United States, $24 to $150 according to tree size), the farmer has increased his receipts and lowered his costs, producing a dual profit increase. But in all this, the profit increase was brought about by change.

The methods program would have a major part in making such changes—whether it be in increasing the receipts or decreasing the expenses, or both. Some functions of a business have more association with changes in one area than in another. This point can be seen in Figure 2.

Manufacturing operations, for example, are geared more toward the cost-reduction avenue to increased profits, while advertising actions are based more on the increased income method. Research and development might have a middle position be-

162

Figure 2. Typical areas of change for different business functions.

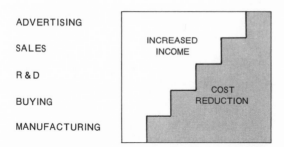

cause it can effect in a major way both new income and cost reductions, through product or material changes. Other functions would also have their own relative positions. For instance, sales might be positioned between advertising and R&D while *buying* might be positioned between manufacturing and R&D.

Because it is usually applied in manufacturing, where cost reduction is particularly appropriate, a formal methods change program is more often known as a cost-reduction plan than as a profit-increase plan. But the methods change program is *not* just a cost-reduction program—it is a profit-increase program brought about by gainful changes. Thus we can ask ourselves, "How much can we change things to produce an increase in profits?" In other words, we would really be asking, "In a year's time, how much would these changes be worth in profit increases to our company?"

The answer to the question is, of course, an annual methods goal, a promise to the company that could produce, for example, millions of dollars of *new* profits beyond last year's profits. And millions of dollars in new profits should be no idle promise! With new funds of this magnitude available, the company would want to make additional major plans. In the May 15, 1972, issue of *Forbes* magazine, Howard Morgens, board chairman of Procter & Gamble Co., said, "If we [P&G] had done everything in fiscal 1971 using the same methods and approaches as in 1970 without making changes, we would have spent $90 million more."

163

An increased profit pledge of multimillion-dollar magnitude is no small commitment. It is tough. To meet the goal, every member of the methods team must constantly search for ways to reduce costs and to increase profits. If a team member does not have 50 percent of his promised goal in the till halfway through the time period, he forces himself more than ever to make *deliberate changes.* He *makes* them happen. He does not *wait* for them to happen. Thus, one can see that a goal, especially a dollar goal in industry, is a must to gain a full advantage of deliberate change.

Deliberate change combined with a goal, worked on a *team basis* in the right atmosphere with *positive recognition,* makes a methods change program far better than any cost-reduction program operating on a "whenever we see any improvements, we make them" basis. This is what is meant by the team-goal methods change program based on the deliberate change concept.

APPLICATION SUMMARY

Three key points—aimed mainly at industrial applications, but usable as well in nonindustrial organizations—have been found vital to a successful methods change program:

1. Form Methods Teams

Organize so that each member of a methods or profit team (especially managers) can spend about 5 percent of his time on deliberate changes. Make certain that the teams have surveyed all the dollars in their areas. (There was a time when most cost-reduction thinking related primarily to wage costs.)

Expand your thinking to include things such as inbound and outbound freight, cost of materials, rent, taxes, and insurance as well as losses, scrap, or material degradings. Plan to use the entire management group. Performance is usually best when all managers participate on a team. Cost reduction is possible wherever dollars are spent. No function should be above participating in profit increase through deliberate change. Keep the responsibility for success where it belongs—on the line organization. The line should retain responsibility for project selection, follow-up, evaluation of progress, and the obvious points of final decision and installation.

2. Establish (Dollar) Goals

Be sure that challenging goals are established. Experience indicates a need for building them democratically, from the first level up. Comparisons stimulating competition among divisions and functional groups are a real incentive for achievement. Be sure that one person (often called a methods coordinator) is assigned to give the program the kind of continuing follow-up and coordination that is necessary for meeting the goal. He or she may conduct or coordinate the methods training (if done by the line supervision) involving material such as Work Simplification, elimination approach, creative thinking, brainstorming, team building, goal setting, even communication skills and others. Training times can range from three half-days to more than a week. The methods coordinator helps with ideas, works on reports, gets answers from the other organizations, and keeps a record of achievements.

When increasing profits by cost reductions, fight the delusion that cost reduction is "cream skimming." Fight the misconception that the next year's goal will be harder to make because of success this year. Remembering that every dollar of cost is a dollar of potential savings, encourage instead the idea that you are really just *starting* to work.

3. Provide Positive Recognition

Taking good methods work for granted will not produce outstanding results. Sincerely done, it is almost impossible to overdo proper recognition. People like to be recognized in the presence of their fellow associates, to be part of a winning team, to feel important even if the recognition is nonmonetary.

CONCLUSION

A methods change program produces one of the most attractive payouts for a continuous organization effort—financial and otherwise. In over 25 years of close experience with one program, I have found that the financial rate of return—using *first-year* savings or profit increases only—has been around 500 percent to 1000 percent before taxes. In other words, five dollars to ten dollars of profit is returned for *every* one dollar spent, including total capital costs of the change. This return is produced by the now over $30,000 profit increase per year per methods team member who spends 5 percent of his time (two hours per week) working on deliberate methods change for gain. For a continuous operation over the years, I know of no other portion of management-type effort that can match this rate of return.

Means and Meanings of Recognition

Parvin S. Titus

Parvin S. Titus is administrator of Cost Improvement Programs and Standards for RCA Corporation in Circleville, Ohio. He has administered Work Simplification, materials handling, and cost improvement programs for RCA and for Henry A. Lurie and Associates. A founding member of the Improvement Institute, he has served as trustee, secretary, vice-president (recognition), and member of the International Advisory Board.

Few would complain of the monotony if all were encouraged to give a sympathetic foreman suggestions for improving the process, and then were made to feel that this would be tied up with an active, well-planned system of recognition. It is monotonous work plus lack of opportunity for personal recognition that makes a bad combination.[1]

The study of human motivation over the past half-century has increased our awareness of the importance of recognition as a motivational force. In his positive theory of human motivation, Maslow discusses two categories of esteem needs—self-esteem and the esteem of other people. Self-esteem is the self-respect based on competence, achievement, independence, and mas-

---

[1] Whiting Williams, *What's on the Worker's Mind*. New York: Charles Scribner's Sons, 1920, p. 196.

tery—a feeling of personal worth. Esteem from others includes respect based on reputation or prestige, status, recognition, attention, and appreciation. A person with adequate self-esteem built upon earned recognition is more confident, capable, and productive.

Research indicates that for most persons, the motivational force of recognition is short-lived and requires frequent reinforcement. It is also interesting to note that failure to receive expected recognition and receipt of unfavorable recognition have been found to produce long-lasting dissatisfaction.[2]

Utilizing Herzberg's motivation−maintenance model, many researchers have studied worker motivation and have found achievement and recognition to be prerequisites to satisfaction of the higher-order needs—esteem and self-actualization. My experience in industry has convinced me that satisfying the social needs is essential to unlock the creativity which earns the highest recognition.

Unfortunately, even in supervisory roles, workers are frequently expected to perform assigned tasks in a highly routine manner. Deviations from prescribed methods are looked upon with great suspicion. Employees are not generally seen as intelligent beings who are capable of self-direction and self-control and who can make a larger contribution. In this atmosphere of disapproval, workers feel insecure and untrusted. With their need for belonging unsatisfied in the working environment, they find their higher-order needs largely inoperative. As Whiting Williams pointed out:

> When the worker becomes in any way convinced as the result of a few deadly demonstrations, that employers as a group are unwilling to reward initiative, loyalty and skill, he gives just enough energy and skill to keep 'the enemy' from discharging him (and he's a wonderful judge of the precise

---

[2] M. Scott Myers, "Who Are Your Motivated Workers?" *Harvard Business Review,* January−February 1964, pp. 82−83.

amount needed for this purpose) and withdraws the reserves of his interests and enthusiasms for more effective and worthwhile application elsewhere.[3]

In most organizations, the latent potential for creative improvement is high, but the environment fails to provide the necessary stimulation and support on a continuing basis. Approval and recognition are needed to set the stage for building self-esteem through achievements which have real meaning for the individual.[4]

RECOGNITION AND PRAISE

Simple praise of continuing routine performance is an accepted supervisory practice. Its potential as a motivator is open to question.

Praise of performance of highly structured, routine tasks—particularly if seen by the worker as poorly designed or meaningless—is unlikely to be viewed by the recipient as earned recognition. Although simply an acknowledgment of approval and friendship, it is also an implied evaluation and it may convey some implied threat. The one evaluated is inveigled to maintain a continuously praiseworthy performance level.[5] As J. Douglas Brown puts it:

> The framing condition of the effective use of praise or criticism in leadership is sincere personal interest in the person to whom it is directed. Genuine interest in and under-

---

[3] Whiting Williams, op. cit., p. 300.
[4] For more on this, see: Raymond E. Miles, "The Affluent Organization," *Harvard Business Review,* May–June 1966, pp. 106 ff.; and Leo B. Moore, "Too Much Management, Too Little Chance," *Harvard Business Review,* January–February 1956, pp. 51 ff.
[5] See Richard E. Farson, "Praise Reappraised," *Harvard Business Review,* September–October 1963, pp. 61 ff.

standing of the recipient permits one to sense the delicate balance of self-confidence and self-doubt that lies in each of us. Praise, when deserved, can go far to tip the balance. Where mutual respect exists, it can reach deep into the conscious and unconscious personality of the recipient.[6]

Performance feedback is recognition. Keeping workers informed of group goals and accomplishments, impending changes, and other facts which may interest or affect them aids workers in recognizing the world they are in and their importance in it. This problem is discussed in the monthly publication of a large bank:

> Few people are self-sufficient. They need appreciation of what they are doing. It may not be public acclaim which is distasteful to some. What everyone needs is understanding of his purpose and effort, and a sharing of this feeling that the work of his hands, whether beautiful or useful, is important.[7]

THE SUGGESTION PROGRAM

"And for his suggestion of an improved method of idler arm adjustment, I'm happy to present this check for $168.62 to Harry Oates." The supervisor shakes hands with Harry; the photographer takes their picture for the plant paper; the crowd disperses. Harry: "168.62! That idea will save them $80,000!"

Jim, Joe, and Jeff (Harry's co-workers): "Where does he get off writing that up? We talked about that for weeks over coffee. It was our idea as much as his!"

---

[6]J. Douglas Brown, *The Human Nature of Organizations.* New York: American Management Associations, 1973, p. 91.
[7]"In the Long Run," Royal Bank of Canada Monthly Letter, Montreal, April 1968, p. 1.

George (an engineer): "Why does he get paid for that? If I hadn't redesigned the assembly, it could never have been done."

Recognition? Yes! Positive motivation? No! Most suggestion plans lead to the kinds of divisive attitudes suggested above. In today's complex organizations, there is rarely one person who can accept full responsibility from ideation to implementation. The suggestor's function is to write his idea, however vague, on paper. It remains for others to evaluate, design, build, install, test, modify, and operate.

The first problem with the suggestion plan as outlined above is that it recognizes only the one person whose name appears on the bottom line. Although I have seen instances where suggesters submitted elaborate drawings, designed and built fixtures, and tested their methods, these are the exception rather than the rule. Most progressive innovations require the cooperative efforts of many persons from many disciplines.

The simplest modification of the suggestion system to combat this problem is to charge the program administrator with the responsibility of ferreting out and recognizing all those who contributed to the successful completion of an improvement. This places a considerable burden on the administrator. It further results in the dilution of the payout to the extent that cash awards are eliminated and token recognition is given to all participants.

A higher order of sophistication is seen in the operation of an employee suggestion system in a plant with a pay plan under which the employee receives an award if the suggestion increases output, and because of the productivity increase, he also gets a pay increase. The reward to the individual worker is substantial, while others using the new method also share through pay increases resulting from their increased productivity. This ties the recognition to the contribution with the award of group increases for group effectiveness.[8]

---

[8] David Sirota, "Productivity Management," *Harvard Business Review,* September–October 1966, p. 115.

TEAM APPROACHES

The inequities, jealousies, and rivalries inherent in the suggestion system approach have given rise to the more equitable team approach in improvement management. Not only do teams accomplish more goals, but they add breadth and depth to recognition.

Through participation in a variety of improvement activities, team members achieve visible results which the individual rarely experiences. A part-originator and a contributor to the completion and successful installation of the whole project, the team member experiences genuine success. This real achievement feeds self-esteem. He receives recognition from his peer team members for his contributions and from his superiors as a member of a successful team. There is nothing quite like the overflowing peer support and goodwill that permeates the locker room of a winning team. That is the goal of team effort: to be successful and to share the resulting bounty.

FORMAL RECOGNITION

Formal methods of recognizing team achievement are extremely diverse, as some organizations have been very ingenious in devising means of recognition. Publicity of all types is employed. Bulletin boards, house organs, newsletters, program bulletins, local newspapers, television, and company annual reports are all used to highlight programs and participants. In-house meetings are often used to recognize individual and group accomplishments. Annual or semiannual dinners may be held at which outstanding groups are recognized and accomplishments recounted. Dinners attended by wives and supervisors of those honored have proved effective in recognition of individuals and small groups.

Opportunities for personal growth and development can be effectively integrated into a recognition system. Visits to other plants and organizations, attendance at professional meetings, and sabbaticals reward the recipient and increase his knowledge and skills.

Visible awards may range from the recognition pin or pen and pencil all the way to merchandise and trips worth hundreds of dollars or more. Such awards bear no relationship to the full value of the individual and group contribution to organizational success. Unlike the monetary reward, there is no issue over the relative size of the reward and the contribution; the potential award was known at the outset.

Other signs of recognition which may be displayed are traveling trophies and banners, reserved parking in the parking lot for a period of time, or tables in the lunchroom. These status symbols may be effective if the participants desire them.

The important point is that participants be recognized publicly and their contribution be acknowledged as important. Arthur Spinanger once commented: "Sincerely done, it is almost impossible to overdo proper recognition. People like to be recognized in the presence of their associates; be a part of a winning team; feel important by being important."[9]

PAY INCREASES AND PROMOTIONS

There is hardly a manager who would not claim that non-negotiated pay increases (other than general or cost-of-living increases) and promotions are given in recognition of performance. The effectiveness of this reward system as a motivator is dependent upon the individual and his perceptions of the goal-reward relationship. What value does the individual place upon the reward? Does his experience tell him that effort on his part will earn him a desired reward?

Money is, after all, an economic and social medium of

[9] Arthur Spinanger, "Increasing Profits through Deliberate Methods Change," Proceedings, Seventh Annual Industrial Engineering Institute, University of California, February 1965, p. 37.

173

exchange. The level of monetary compensation speaks to the individual and to the outside world of his value and status in the organization and society. The failure of wages to permit satisfaction of survival needs or to match the individual's appraisal of his worth is a source of job dissatisfaction.

A satisfactory wage level is not fixed. Erosion of money value, continuing negotiation of increases, and growing desires for goods and services lead people to seek increased compensation for their labors. Meritorious performance is certainly the most valid justification for such increases.

As a form of recognition, however, pay increases have a number of shortcomings. They are generally granted on the basis of performance or accomplishment over time. Hence they are not timely feedback or recognition of achievement. One could not expect an organization to continually bestow large increases; recognition through frequent small ones soon would become meaningless.

Pay increases are also not usually a visible reward. Secrecy typically surrounds the payroll of most organizations. Only through conspicuous consumption can one display the reward of a pay increase. And if the recipient has no psychological wants which money will satisfy, it is an empty reward. Some organizations frequently bestow pay increases on workers despite specific nonperformance. Seniority and not rocking the boat are rewarded with increases as large as or larger than those given to creative improvement.

Specific contributions tend to fade from memory over time. To preserve them, a simple citation recounting the causes for recognition should be sent to the recipient and to his or her superior, and a copy inserted in the employee record. Although no guarantee of equity in pay increases and promotions, this does retell the achievements to all who may consult the record.

As a form of recognition, promotions appear to provide greater psychological advantage than raises. Promotion offers opportunity for further growth, increased independence, and prestige as well as financial gain. A rise in status is apparent on the organization chart and in the community. It connotes advanced economic status, overcoming the temporary aspect of the wage increase alone. Here again, however, the reward occurs considerably after the achievement. Also, promotion cannot regularly be used as reinforcement. The typical hierarchical organization triangle graphically illustrates the impossibility of limitless recognition through promotion.

Although continued excellence on the worker's part will often justify the reward and encourage further recognition, an average or marginally competent performance by recipients of the reward may harm the organization and rob these employees of the very respect and self-esteem that resulted from their achievements.

CONCLUSION

Today's management faces a workforce whose physiological and safety needs are essentially satisfied. Social and egoistic needs are the wellsprings of motivation in modern industrial nations.

Opportunities for satisfaction of the higher-order needs are keenly sought throughout society, but unfortunately they are more easily found outside the workplace than within it. To maximize the potential of the worker, the working environment must provide similar opportunities. As McGregor noted: ". . . under proper conditions, unimagined resources of creative human energy could become available within the organizational setting." [10]

Timely recognition of achievement is a primary qualification. Belief in the creative potential of people and a desire to use it are necessary conditions. A fairly administered, universally known recognition system demonstrates this belief. The classical employee suggestion system and percent-of-savings cash awards have been relatively ineffective. Pay increases for true merit usually lack necessary timeliness and visibility. Promotion is the highest form of recognition, but its limitations require other forms to fulfill day-to-day needs.

---

[10] Douglas McGregor, Fifth Anniversary Convocation of the School of Industrial Management, MIT, Cambridge, Mass., April 9, 1957.

Recognition of team effort correlates best with the realities of today's organizations. By helping to reach the objective, all participants reinforce their sense of personal worth. Recognition of peers and superiors gives real meaning to the accomplishment.

Rewards given in recognition for achievement are limited only by the imagination. The reward system must allow for individual differences in reward preference. Like organizations, individuals grow and change. Dynamic people are not stimulated by static systems.

Recognition through a system of desirable rewards, presented in a timely fashion and fairly administered, stimulate individual and group effort toward the achievement of personal and organization goals.

Career
Identity
Crisis

Ben S. Graham, Jr.

Ben S. Graham, Jr., Ph.D., president of The Ben Graham Corporation (Tipp City, Ohio), strongly influenced by his father's innovative work, has expanded the repertoire of techniques applicable to paperwork improvement and, through his behavioral science research, has advanced management's understanding of the participative process in the office environment.

Where work is performed by healthy growing human beings, it is natural to include as a part of the job, its creative management and improvement.

Career identity develops when a person immerses himself in a job and masters it. If he sits back waiting to find out who he is, he will find little. *Identity is not discovered—it is built.* Human beings grow to adulthood with little effort on their own part. With maturity this situation changes and, in order to survive, each person must build and maintain an adult identity.

Identity building should be a lifelong process. Both individuals and organizations will find it much easier to keep identities growing if they deal with life segments, each one to include preparation, mastery, and then moving on to a new challenge.

Previously appeared in Danish as "Karriereidentitetens Krise," in *MANagement 83*, C. A. Oberg (ed.), Oberg-ODC, Dalgas 20, DK 2000 Copenhagen, 1972.

The idea of finding and fixing on one career identity for life is strongly rooted in our traditions. However, technology has made many of these lifelong identities narrow and stifling. Now it is up to man to adapt and, instead of being pigeonholed by education, to use education to build identities worthy of man.

Multiple careers are needed in many cases to replace traditional lifelong careers. Societies and the organizations of which they are composed cannot expect to prosper if their people are failing. There are forces at work in Western civilization which are bringing on increasing incidence of individual failure. These forces are related to technological change and are reinforced by some of our most deeply held values.

THE FORCES AT WORK

Education has produced the basic underlying force. Specifically, the force is generated by the increasing portions of the population who are receiving formal education and continuing on to each level of higher education. These people constitute a highly literate population, increasingly competent with numbers and conversant with scientific phenomena.

This educated population has, in turn, generated secondary forces by rapidly increasing the body of knowledge available to man and using that knowledge innovatively to alter most of our ways of doing work. Wherever we look, we see the work of the world being done in ways which were not available a generation ago, a decade ago, or even a week ago. Furthermore, because of the increasing numbers of people who are being educated, to the extent that they are able to participate in innovation, this rate of change steadily climbs.

These underlying forces are not new. They have been mounting for centuries and recently in such magnitude that a new phenomenon dominates the arena of career identity. I will call it "turbulent technology" and describe it as a situation where *methods of work are changing at a pace and in a manner that exceeds the capacity of society to adjust.*

178

In turbulent technology, individuals find it more and more difficult to establish and sustain their career identities. This tends to generate a counterforce, as many individuals and groups feel compelled to reverse the processes of education and innovation.

We must reject that alternative. It represents a regression which is no more healthy in society than it is in an adult individual who reacts to frustrations by pretending not to be an adult and reverting to childish behavior. Society is faced with an adult problem, the problem of conducting itself in a fashion in which educated people can thrive. It serves no useful purpose to blame education and knowledge and it is totally reprehensible for society to avoid the issue altogether by dividing up into groups (men, women; young, old; ethnic groups; geographic groups), each blaming the other. *Rather than exhausting our energies in blame, we must turn those energies to directing technology toward the benefit of mankind.*

VALUES REINFORCING THE FORCES OF TURBULENCE

Whenever a society continues along a given course for more than a few years, it is safe to assume that that course is consistent with important values, widely held within that society. In this case it is somewhat ironic that some of man's highest values have sustained processes which are now making life quite uncomfortable. Here are some of them:

1. Respect for knowledge and education and a desire to make them available throughout society.
2. The conviction that each person should have a chance to develop toward his or her potential.
3. An inclination that young people should not be pressed into career choice but should be free to follow directions which are personally important.
4. A conviction held by many parents that they should encourage their children to seek higher educations and loftier careers than they reached themselves.

179

PREPARATION FOR CAREER

As a result of these forces and values, we have produced a world where people have difficulty looking ahead. The future appears vague and tentative and, although it includes many possibilities, they are so indistinct that they seem to blend into a single picture dominated by uncertainty.

The vagueness of tomorrow is an extension of the vagueness of today. Many roles in society are so new that even the people filling them do not understand them well enough to explain them. It seems there is little we can do to prepare new people to fill them.

By contrast, in more primitive societies, the preparation for a career identity usually began in early childhood and by the time a young person reached adulthood he had few doubts concerning his work. Not long ago, in some societies many parents even gave their children a career identity along with the family name. For instance, in English, names like Shepherd, Cooper, Barber, Baker, Farmer, Fisher, etc., all designated careers and just as the names were passed on from one generation to another, the bearers of the names continued to do the work their names described. Parents spent their years of child-rearing preparing their children for work which they, in turn, had been prepared for since their own childhoods. This element of childhood preparation for a lifelong career is mostly gone from Western society today. Part of our current failure rate may be because of this.

FAILURES IN ESTABLISHING IDENTITY

Looking ahead at a variety of vague and rapidly changing careers, many young people are justifiably hesitant. Rather than choosing a career, they hold back as if intuitively they know that once they begin there will be little chance of turning back. Some hold back completely, embarking on no career. Others enter a career tentatively, in body but not in mind. They do not really become involved but rather go through the motions of work while waiting for something better to come along. In neither case is an effective career identity established.

The key factor at the outset of identity building is commitment, but the situation young people find themselves in today discourages commitment. In the face of turbulence, transience, and vagueness, armed with values which encourage advanced education and personal choice but with little childhood preparation for any specific career, they think it prudent to defer this decision, pursue an advanced education or other forms of unique experience, and wait for the "right job" to come along.

Unfortunately, the sequence of behaviors which lead to adult socialization cannot be postponed. If the young people confine their experience to academia, they will establish identities made up of theory without substance. If they withdraw to wander across the country or enter into some sort of communal life, they will find meanings that are apt to include somewhat exaggerated hostilities toward the society they are avoiding. If they enter a career half-heartedly, their identities will be fed by the trivia they pick up through their uninspired performances.

The key point is that identity formation cannot be postponed: it is formed out of whatever meanings are available as the young person enters adulthood. If there is little or no firsthand career substance out of which to form it, there will be little or no career identity.

The longer these people postpone the establishment of a career identity, the less chance they will have of doing so effectively. Those who begin work indifferently will, through their uninspired performances, establish themselves as unimaginative and unpromising, thus destroying their chances of pursuing better opportunities. They will find that the work gradually becomes more distasteful, and they will tend to blame the organization and its authorities. Eventually they will either move someplace else and try to start over, or resign themselves to meager careers.

Those who hold out and do not start careers can watch their mundane contemporaries and be pleased that they didn't allow this to happen to them. However, they are not much better off. They find many reasons to fault society and to justify their not

181

being a part of it. Gradually the faultfinding turns to hostility and leads to antisocial behaviors which, depending on how repugnant they are to society, make it increasingly difficult for these people to ever move toward establishing a career within society.

FAILURE OF EFFECTIVE IDENTITIES

The problems of young people establishing career identities are often bizarre, and frequently appear in newspaper headlines. By comparison, the failures of existing career identities are unimposing and anonymous. Yet, of the two, the latter pose the greater problem for society, for they occur within society itself. They are fundamental, the direct result of the forces working within society. By comparison, not joining society is secondary.

The effective career identity is built as follows. First there is commitment to the career, which leads to immersion. Then—through hours, weeks, and months of involvement—the person accumulates skills and personal meanings which constitute a career identity. During this time the person is oblivious to himself and to what is going on around him. His attention is on the activity at hand. He becomes more and more deeply involved in subtle details of the work, which are unknown to people who have not actually done the work. In this sense the work becomes increasingly private.

The process of mastery is an intense, lonely pursuit of excellence accompanied by rich nourishment of a growing identity. Lost in the work, the person grows as his senses incorporate firsthand experience, which accumulates to build substantial personal meaning.

However, this process can also abort. A lot depends on where the person is immersed and on how much substance is to be found there. When a person has mastered all there is to be found in a job, he can no longer grow. In some jobs this occurs appallingly soon after the job is first entered. Then if the job cannot be expanded or the person cannot move into another, the quality of his career identity begins to deteriorate.

Involvement is gradually replaced by boredom and indifference. Enthusiasm wanes and the person ceases to keep up with the changing requirements of the work. Performance becomes lackluster. The person learns to insulate himself from situations which require alert attention. In time the work becomes almost hypnotic, as everything within it is reduced to routine that requires no thought. What was once exciting now holds no interest at all.

The person is no longer alive on the job in the sense of having a wholesome, vital career identity. He may become very active in other segments of his life, such as hobbies, family, community affairs, religion, or sports, and all this can be fine, as it is healthy for people to develop balanced identities. However, it is a shame that close to one-fourth of a person's life is spent in meaningless activity. Worse yet, this type of activity gradually erodes a person's capacity for identity growth.

Consider the young man vigorously setting out to master a career. We look at him again in his mid-thirties and find him performing in a routine, monotonous fashion with no expectation of further change until retirement. Later, at sixty-five, he has had thirty years of practice at being dead on the job and, when enforced retirement makes it official, he obligingly dies. Why? Because for years his feeble career identity has given him just enough personal meaning to sustain life. When this is removed he finds his capacity for replacing it no longer exists. If he could find meaning and purpose in other areas he could survive. However, actuarial statistics bear mute testimony to the fact that many retirees are unable to do this.

The plight of all too many people at retirement age is unpardonable. Worse yet are the years of wasted life which preceded retirement, beginning when the career identity growth ceased. If society can correct this problem, most of the other problems associated with career identity will be relieved.

MULTIPLE CAREERS

The most important single step we must take to avert identity failure is for society in general to *replace the traditional notion of preparation for a job for life* with ideas that are more appropriate for the complex and changing world we have built. There are some jobs that are large and varied enough to nourish an identity for life. However, more and more, we are creating narrow specialties that do not promote the growth of jobholders over the span of their working lives. When they find themselves in jobs which have run out of room for growth, some people are able to move on to other jobs. However, many cannot do this, and these are the people we must concern ourselves with. They represent a dangerously increasing portion of society. First we must assess each job in terms of how long it can remain healthy and then set that period as the 'tour' for the job (an appropriate period of time for a person to hold the job). This will mean that people entering jobs will know how long they can expect to be in them. After that, they will move into something else. For management, the focus of their organization efforts will change from a relatively static treatment of positions to a more dynamic management of the flow of human energy through jobs. In fact, the idea of keeping turnover low will be replaced by an idea of keeping turnover at a healthy level appropriate for each job.

Many people who are alive today will, we hope, experience mastery in several job experiences—perhaps five, six, even seven—during their lives. These experiences may be sequential, each building on the previous ones in a logical succession of increasing skills and responsibilities, or they may be as unrelated as being an athlete at one time, an artist at another, and a salesman at another. The key point is that people will continue to find work in which they can grow. This will keep them involved and vital and, in turn, will be reflected in their performances.

CAREER PATHS

Some multiple career paths will be developed without any drastic departure from what managers have been doing for years. There will be a little more attention to building career bridges which provide logical exits from work which has ceased to encourage growth into other areas where people can continue to grow. Special attention will be given to dead-end jobs and some form of exit provided for each.

After these career paths have been located, there is the important task of keeping the paths open and people moving through them. This means we cannot allow individuals to wedge themselves into positions and hold up those who are following them. When this happens it is necessary to "pull the plug" before a chain reaction occurs with damaging effect to all those careers that are delayed. When we wait for enforced retirement to do this for us, we risk much. The time limits placed on jobs along career paths must be worked out and maintained to provide a healthy balanced flow.

Dramatic Career Changes

It is hardly feasible, however, to expect that career paths within organizations will be adequate to meet all of the demands of a turbulent society. We will also have to anticipate and prepare for a steadily increasing number of abrupt and unrelated career changes. In this, the management task is considerably more complex. It will require counseling to help people work out satisfactory and realistic career objectives. It will require placement assistance and it will require so much continuing education that the time will come when people no longer associate education with youth.

Why should organizations go to all of this trouble? Because it will help them to prosper. People who are turning in uninspired performances do not add as much to an organization's success as those who are alive and growing. It is worthwhile to try to maximize the percentage of people who are making vital contributions.

This requires moving some people out when their contributions are no longer adequate. Managers have often been reluctant to do this out of sympathy and respect for the past performances of the employee. Employers have carried employees without always realizing that the effect on the employee is

185

usually to lock him permanently into a position in which he will continue to perform unsatisfactorily.

It is to the advantage of both the organization and the individual to find alternatives where people can be useful and grow in new ways.

We often give up on people too soon. We see a person performing unimpressively and we assume that is all we can expect from him. How shortsighted this is! Few people ever approach their potentials, but many burn out, not because they have done all that they could possibly do, but because they have done all that was available. They are bored—they need something different if they are to come alive again, and they need it before they have wasted away so long that they are unable to start again.

Society is in need of a vital new skill. We need to be able to catch people when they have completely mastered their work, while their career identities are still healthy but are just beginning to deteriorate. Then we need to help them to find new substance for self-growth.

Not an Invitation to Job Hopping

If this sounds like a world where people are constantly being trained but are never staying around to perform, this is wrong. The idea of a person having several careers during a lifetime is not an invitation to irresponsible job hopping.

The key to individual and organizational fulfillment is *mastery*. Mastery follows commitment. It also follows formal training, which is not a part of mastery. Mastery occurs during the period of time when a person is actually involved in the work itself. He has given himself over fully to the job. By comparison, training provides only superficial experience like that of a spectator who often thinks he knows what is going on but hasn't really done it.

The idea underlying a series of careers is that a person commits himself fully to one, plunges into it, masters it, becomes it, and then—when it is no longer nourishing—moves on. Each

186

new commitment should be for a significant time, a portion of life, but not all of life.

IMPACTS OF MULTIPLE CAREERS

It should be much easier for many young people to commit themselves to careers if they don't have to make the commitment for life. The fact that each commitment is for only a portion of life should relieve some anxiety and allow them to relax and give themselves to the job in the manner necessary to master it. However, they must be confident that they will not end up trapped, and we must not disappoint them.

Multiple careers will also lead to improvement in the quality of individual life planning. Young people will not simply rush into careers and, before long, find themselves locked into meaningless and hopeless existences. Too much of life today is governed by immature decisions that become needlessly irreversible. As more options become available, more people will be able to plan fulfilling lives.

There should also be improvement in the quality of childhood preparation for careers when parents themselves are engaged in lifelong career growth. An awkward period in the evolution of mankind, when relatively uneducated parents were unable to help their more educated children, will pass. As parents build stronger, richer identities, they will have more to offer to their children, who in turn will have more to offer theirs. And in an altogether new fashion the childhood preparation for a career, which is now missing, will be restored. It will not be for specific careers, as in primitive societies. However, as young people grow up watching parents moving in and out of several periods of mastery, they will see examples that will give them the kind of preparation they need.

Another impact of multiple careers will be to place renewed emphasis on building meaning and purpose into work. Work which offers no challenge will gradually be eliminated through

187

automated techniques. It will be performed by equipment. By contrast, where work is to be performed by healthy, growing human beings, it will seem natural to include, as a part of the job, its creative management and improvement. This will involve taking advantage of the unique firsthand experience of the people who are actively mastering the work. They will manage and improve the methods of their own jobs and they will work with other masters to manage and redesign systems which involve many jobs.

Perhaps one of the most refreshing impacts of multiple careers will be that in time we will be able to look back on the brutal practice of enforced retirement (a primitive system for getting rid of people rendered useless by society), but we will no longer be compelled to look forward to it. In a society where human beings grow throughout life, the thought of an arbitrary age when work performances end will seem ridiculous.

Selected Readings

Bennis, Warren G., Benne, Kenneth D., and Chin, Robert. *The Planning of Change.* 3rd ed. New York: Holt, Rinehart & Winston, 1976.

Bennis, Warren B., and Schein, Edgar H. *Leadership and Motivation, Essays of Douglas McGregor.* Cambridge, Mass.: MIT Press, 1966.

Ford, Robert N. *Motivation Through the Work Itself.* New York: American Management Association, 1969.

Foulkes, Fred K. *Creating More Meaningful Work.* New York: American Management Association, 1969.

Gardner, John W. *Self-Renewal—The Individual and the Innovative Society.* New York: Harper & Row, 1965.

Kobayaski, Shigeru. *Creative Management.* New York: American Management Association, 1971.

Lehrer, Robert N. *Work Simplification.* Englewood Cliffs, N.J.: Prentice-Hall, 1967.

Likert, Rensis. *Human Organization, Its Management and Value.* New York: McGraw-Hill, 1967.

Mali, Paul. *Improving Total Productivity.* New York: Wiley Interscience, 1978.

Maslow, Abraham H. *Eupsychian Management.* Homewood, Ill.: Richard D. Irwin, 1965.

Myers, M. Scott. *Every Employee a Manager.* New York: McGraw-Hill, 1970.

Myers, M. Scott. *Managing Without Unions.* Reading, Mass.: Addison-Wesley, 1976.

Myers, M. Scott. *Managing With Unions.* Reading, Mass.: Addison-Wesley, 1978.

Vough, Clair F., and Asbell, B. *Tapping the Human Resource: A Strategy for Productivity.* New York: American Management Association, 1975.

Index

191

Eastman Kodak, 17, 19
employees
    career paths for, 185–186
    responsibilities of, 9–11
    see also workers
engineering, 21–22
executives
    change in responsibilities of, 13–14
    reflectivity by, 80–81
expenses, deliberate methods changes for, 161–163

Farson, Richard E., 169n.
fear, as motivation, 56
feedback
    pay increases as, 174
    recognition as, 170
    in team approach, 150
films, 18–20, 50–51
five-step pattern for problem solving, 48–53
flow-process charts, 35
follow-throughs, in paperwork simplification, 41–42
Ford, Robert N., 189
foremen, *see* supervisors
forms control, 42–43
Fosdick, Harry Emerson, 62
Foulkes, Fred K., 189
Fulton, Robert, 86

gains, deliberate methods changes for, 161–164
Gantt, Henry K., 77
Gardner, B. B., 102
Gardner, John W., 189
Gellerman, Saul W., 102
Germany, 162

Gilbreth, Frank, 19, 21, 30
    motion study by, 35
Gilbreth, Lillian M., 19, 30, 31, 77, 102
    motion study by, 35
    on role of management, 21–29
Globe, Frank, 137
goals
    in deliberate methods change, 160–161, 165
    in paperwork simplification, 30–31, 43–46
    of workers, 112–113
Goldberg, Rube, 34
Gompers, Samuel, 109
Goodwin, Herbert F., 102
    on management of improvement, 65–83
Graham, Ben S., Sr., 102
    on paperwork simplification, 30–47
Graham, Ben S., Jr., on career identity crises, 177–188
groups
    initiation of, 94–96
    problems appropriate for, 98–100
    in team approach to improvement, 145–154
    techniques of action in, 92–94
    timing of actions of, 97–98
    see also teams

Haire, Mason, 102
Hawthorne studies, 131
Hayes, John J., 103
Haywood, William, 109
Herzberg, Frederick, 168
hobos, 59
homemaking, 12, 26

Hoover, Herbert, 27
horizontal teams, 149
housewives, as "home managers," 12
H. P. Hood and Sons, 49
human nature, 28

ideation, 139
identity crises, 177–188
improvement
  change and innovation for, 128
  comparison of programs for, 139–154
  management of, 65–83, 84–101
improvement management, 71–82
industrial engineers, 19
industry, change in work of, 14–15
incentives, 47
innovation
  human energy for, 127–138
  see also change
Ishikawa, Kaoru, 136–137

Japan, 135–137
job enrichment
  in "every worker as manager approach," 120–122
  management approach to, 124–126
jobholder approach to job restructuring, 120–122
jobs
  as measurement of usefulness, 57–59
  multiple careers and, 178, 186–188
  program solving in, 50–52
  restructuring of, 120–126

turnover in, 184
  see also work
job security, 77

Kettering, Charles, 50
knowledge, of ruling class, 107–108
Kobayaski, Shigeru, 189

labor
  convergence between management and, 111–112
  see also unions; workers
Lasieur, Fred G., 102
Lehrer, Robert N., 189
Likert, Rensis, 102, 189
Lincoln, James F., 102
line workers
  in deliberate methods change, 165
  improvement responsibilities of, 89
lower class, 107–108

McGregor, Douglas, 68, 103, 175
machine operators, see operators, machine
McPherson, Joe, 48
Maier, Norman R. F., 103
Mali, Paul, 189
management
  change in, 84–101
  convergence between workers and, 111–112
  L. Gilbreth on role of, 21–29
  of improvement, 65–83
  innovation and, 129–130
  paperwork simplification and, 37, 42, 44–45
  skills needed, in general, 12–13

193

194

supervisors (continued)
    in job enrichment planning,
        125–126
    meaningful role of, 117–118
    responsibilities of, 9–11
    union stewards and, 119–120

task force approach to job restruc-
    turing, 122–124
Taylor, Frederick W., 17, 77
teams
    in deliberate methods change,
        160–161, 164–165
    improvement programs based
        on, 139–140, 145–154
    recognition in, 172
    see also groups
teamwork
    creative, 77–79
    for improvement, 92–93
technology, 178–179
television
    advertising on, 131–132
    workers' knowledge and, 110–
        111
Texas Instruments Company, 134,
    135
Thompson, Elihu, 7
time and motion studies, 18–19
Titus, Parvin S.
    on five steps to improvement,
        48–53
    on recognition, 167–176
training, in paperwork simplifica-
    tion, 40–41
turnover, 184
two-class system, 107–109

unemployment, 23

unions
    American class system and, 109
    in job enrichment planning, 125
    organized around grievances, 60
    stewards of, 119–120

Vanderbilt, Cornelius, 86
vertical teams, 149
videotapes, 20, 50
volunteer jobs, 27
Vough, Clair F., 189

wages, 174
waste, paperwork simplification for
    reduction in, 30–47
Weaver, Richard F., on comparison
    of improvement programs,
        139–154
Westinghouse, George, 86
Williams, Whiting, 75, 103
    on employee dissatisfaction,
        168–169
    on recognition, 167
    on wants of workers, 54–64
work
    simplicity in, 34–36
    smooth flow of, 33–34
    see also jobs
workers
    changing perspective of, 109–
        110
    convergence between manage-
        ment and, 111–112
    improvement responsibilities of,
        89
    job dissatisfaction of, 118–119
    as managers, 114, 120–122
    personal goals of, 112–113
    wants of, 54–64
    working class, 108–109